...ayed in th...

Shootout

NEW ISLAND

Shootout

The Battle for
St Stephen's Green, 1916

Paul O'Brien

1916 IN FOCUS

SHOOTOUT
First published 2013
by New Island
2 Brookside
Dundrum Road
Dublin 14
www.newisland.ie

P/B   ISBN: 978-1-84840-211-9
ePub   ISBN: 978-1-84840-239-3
emobi   ISBN: 978-1-84840-240-9

Typeset by Mariel Deegan
Book design by Mariel Deegan
Cover image Robert McDonough, West Cork Flying Column, 2008
Printed by Bell & Bain Ltd, UK

New Island received financial assistance from
The Arts Council (An Comhairle Ealaíon), Dublin, Ireland

This book is dedicated to the men and women of the Irish Citizen Army.

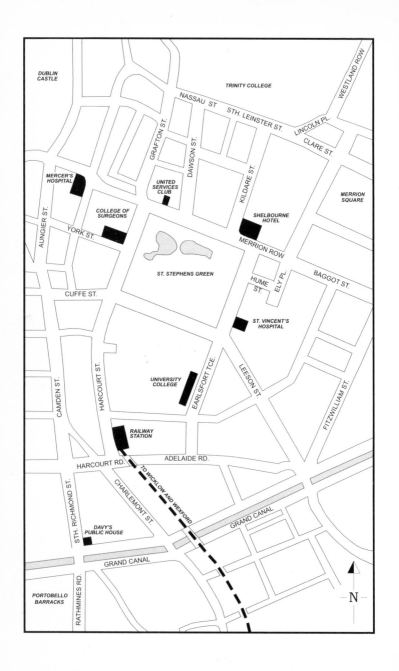

Contents

Acknowledgements

I owe a particular debt of gratitude to Fiach O'Broin and to my wife Marian who encouraged me to explore and examine this battle in detail.

For their professional advice and for reading the initial drafts, I would like to thank Sergeant Wayne Fitzgerald, Barrister John McGuiggan and Dr Mary Montaut.

I am indebted to Sue Sutton for her research in the British Military Archives at Kew in London, to Elizabeth Gillis and James Langton for research on the Irish Volunteers and Citizen Army and to Michael Poole for information on his family.

I would like to express my thanks to Nuala Canny of the Library of the Office of Public Works, the staff of the National Library and the Staff of the Historic Properties section of the O.P.W.

I am most grateful to Commandant Padraic Kennedy, Lisa Dolan, Noelle Grothier and all the staff of Military Archives in Dublin, Anne Marie Ryan in Kilmainham Gaol Archives, Ed Penrose of the Irish Labour History Society and Mary O'Doherty of the Royal College of Surgeons.

For bringing the battle to life, thanks are due to Gerry Woods for an excellent map.

A special word of thanks to Denis O'Brien at the Shelbourne Hotel who was so generous with his time.

I would like to thank the following for Information, their assistance, encouragement and advice: Henry Fairbrother, Ray Bateson, Joanna Bruck, David Grant, Darren O'Brien, Michael Cahill, Tommy Galvin, Micheál O'Doibhlín and my parents Thomas and Rita.

Many thanks to all at New Island Books, especially Eoin Purcell and Dr Justin Corfield for their continued support.

In researching this book I consulted many soldiers, both at home and abroad, serving and retired. Having been given a military scenario, they assisted me in meticulously working out each detail of attack and defence thus enabling me to re-evaluate the strategy and tactics of this battle. I am grateful to them all.

There are many people who helped with this book and in naming some of them I can only apologise to those who I fear I may have indirectly forgotten and I would like to invite them to make me aware of any omissions or relevant information that may be included in any future updated edition.

The Irish Citizen Army were a separate organisation to that of the Irish Volunteers. However, throughout this work, to distinguish Republican forces from British forces, I have referred to members of the Irish Citizen Army as Volunteers.

Paul O'Brien
Dublin, April 2013
paulobrienauthor.ie

Foreword

'The battlefield is a scene of constant chaos. The winner will be the one that controls that chaos, both his own and the enemy's.'[1]

The terrain upon which military engagements occur can go a long way towards determining their outcome, and military commanders select their battlegrounds with care. In some circumstances, however, a commander will be assigned an area of operations that they must then secure and hold against enemy forces. This, more often than not, is a difficult task for the commanding officer, who will need to draw upon every skill he possesses to succeed in his mission.

As one strolls through St Stephen's Green, in the heart of Dublin city, it is difficult to imagine that this tranquil public park was once the scene of a weeklong gun battle.

On Easter Monday, 24 April 1916, the Irish Citizen Army's primary objective was to occupy and hold the public park of St Stephen's Green. Located on the South Side of Dublin city, this twenty-two acre site was to be used as a depot area. It had been envisaged that as news of the insurrection spread throughout the country, men, weapons and transport would converge on the city. From the Green, strategic deployments of men and materials could be made. This position was also considered a central location with a fresh water supply. James Connolly, Commander-in-Chief of the Irish Citizen Army, knew that in urban combat, essential services would be disrupted and any reserves he could hold would place him on a better footing in the coming battles.

A number of roads intersected in this area, and by securing these points, Volunteer forces could control traffic in and out of the area of operations. Securing the Green and its surrounds would also act as a link between the 2nd Battalion of the Irish Volunteers in Jacob's Biscuit Factory on Aungier Street and the 3rd Battalion, Irish Volunteers located in Boland's Bakery in Ringsend.

The officer entrusted to carry out operations in this area was Commandant Michael Mallin. Born in Dublin in 1874, Commandant Mallin was an experienced soldier, having served fourteen years in the British Army, many of them overseas. On his return to Ireland he became a silk weaver and an active trade unionist, and subsequently Secretary to the Silk Weavers' Union. In 1913 he joined the ranks of the Irish Citizen Army, where his military ability was noted by James Connolly, who promoted Mallin to the rank of Chief of Staff of the ICA. Respected and admired by his men, Mallin was a dedicated and competent officer.

Second in command of Mallin's unit was Captain Christopher (Kit) Poole. Born in Dublin into a strong nationalist family in 1875, Poole served in the British Army during the Boer War. On joining the Irish Citizen Army his military experience was noted, and he was promoted to the rank of Captain.[2]

Both of these officers and their men had been involved in an industrial dispute in 1913. 'The Lockout', as it was to become known, was a dispute that spread throughout Dublin city involving 20,000 employees and their 80,000 dependents. They were locked out of their workplaces in a bitter struggle with employers for union recognition and survival. During this turbulent period, union leaders Jim Larkin and James Connolly raised a Citizens' Army in order to defend workers from police brutality. By January 1914, it was evident that the workers had lost the dispute. Lacking the resources for a prolonged campaign, many workers drifted back to work on the employers' terms. In the aftermath of the Lockout, Connolly continued to maintain the Irish Citizen Army, believing that an Irish Workers' Republic could be achieved through armed insurrection and that the Irish Citizen Army was the instrument for gaining that republic. A group of nationalists, however, planned a similar operation.

On 19 January 1916, James Connolly met with members of the Military Council of the Irish Volunteers. At this meeting the Military Council, consisting of Patrick Pearse, Joseph Plunkett and Seán McDermott, informed Connolly of their planned insurrection and the landing of a shipment of German arms and munitions. James Connolly was offered an alliance between his organisation and that of the Irish Volunteers if he postponed his planned uprising. He accepted their offer, knowing that a larger and better-equipped force could achieve more.[3]

Joseph Plunkett and James Connolly drew up the final plans for the Rising incorporating a number of tactics for urban warfare. The defending units had a detailed knowledge of their areas that included the layout of the buildings that they were to occupy. The chosen positions were mutually supporting, and provided the Volunteers with excellent fields of fire. Both senior officers knew that St Stephen's Green was a strategic location that needed to be taken, though it would be difficult to hold.

While the Military Council fixed the date of the insurrection for Easter Sunday 23 April 1916, it would be twenty-four hours later, on Monday 24 April, when the insurrection would finally take place.

The battles that evolved in and around St Stephen's Green and Dublin Castle – the areas controlled by the ICA – pose a number of questions to the student of military history. In relation to British tactics, questions arise in relation to the military strategy employed by the British Army, and in particular why Brigadier General W.H.M. Lowe opted for the tactic of containment of ICA positions when they could have easily been overrun earlier that week.

The actions of the Irish Citizen Army and its commanders during Easter week 1916 are more controversial still. What were the reasons behind the occupation of a public park in the centre of Dublin city? What were the effects of Eoin MacNeill's countermanding order on the ICA, and did it make the plan of occupying the Green redundant? Why did Mallin fail to occupy key positions that were considered a threat to his area of operations? Were the tactics he employed in the park suitable, and why did he opt for a defensive strategy for the remainder of Easter week?

Considered by many to be insignificant, the battle that erupted in this green oasis and its fashionable surroundings was to become one of the landmarks of the fight for Irish independence. What follows is the story of 1916 and the Battle for St Stephen's Green.

Chapter 1

Easter Monday 24 April, 1916: Morning

At 11.30 hours on the morning of Easter Monday 24 April 1916, Commandant Michael Mallin of the Irish Citizen Army (ICA) emerged from ICA headquarters at Liberty Hall.

From the steps of the building, Commandant Mallin inspected his force. Of an estimated four hundred men within the Irish Citizen Army only two hundred and twenty had mobilised, many of them attired in their distinctive bottle-green uniforms and slouch hats. They were armed with a variety of weapons that included Lee Enfield's, Martini carbines and Mauser rifles, as well as a number of shotguns. The Officers and Non-Commissioned Officers carried Webley revolvers and Mauser automatic pistols.

The Rising that had been scheduled for the previous day, Sunday 23 April, had been postponed due to a countermanding order issued by Eoin MacNeill. A member of the supreme council of the Irish Republican Brotherhood (IRB), MacNeill withdrew his support for the Rising having heard that Roger Casement had been arrested and that the *Aud,* a ship laden with arms and ammunition, had been intercepted by the Royal Navy. Not only was the rescinding order published in the national press, but it was also distributed by courier throughout the rest of the country. Though the planned mobilisation was postponed on Sunday, the military council of the IRB decided to go ahead and ordered a mobilisation for the following day, Easter Monday. The Irish Citizen Army were significantly understrength, as were the Irish Volunteers, and any hope of the ranks of the ICA being strengthened by Volunteer units dissipated with MacNeill's countermanding order. Mallin knew that the task ahead would be difficult, and that his small force was inadequate to complete the mission he had been assigned.

While the main plan involved taking St Stephen's Green, it also incorporated the occupation of a number of outer posts that were intended to prevent or delay the advance of British forces towards the Green or into the city. Captain Richard McCormack was ordered to take a force of forty-five men and occupy Harcourt Street Railway Terminus and secure the immediate area. His orders were to impede British troop movements until the Green and all city centre positions had been manned and secured. He was then to fall back and reinforce those in the Green.

Captain Seán Connolly with a special detachment of thirty members of the ICA would secure City Hall, and from this position contain Crown forces within Dublin Castle and halt any advance by the enemy towards the centre of the city. This delaying tactic would enable other units to secure their positions before British troops could launch a concerted counter-attack.

Unlike many of the other organisations of that time, women were welcomed into the ranks of the Irish Citizen Army. Prevailing social values and sexual stereotypes were rejected, as women received the same training as their male counterparts. Holding the rank of Captain, Dr Kathleen Lynn was the Chief Medical Officer in the Irish Citizen Army. She had been detailed to join Seán Connolly's unit at City Hall. A motorcar and driver were provided to transport Dr Lynn and her medical supplies to the area of operations. Accompanying the doctor was Countess Constance Markievicz. A radical nationalist, she held the rank of lieutenant, but was later to receive a field commission to the rank of Vice Commandant.

At 11.40 hours, Captain Poole ordered bugler William Oman to sound the command to fall in at Beresford Place outside Liberty Hall. Four hundred members of the Irish Volunteers, Irish Citizen Army and other republican organisations mustered and made ready to move out.

The Irish Citizen Army were among the first units to march off, with Captain McCormack's section heading towards Harcourt Street Railway Terminus. Minutes later, Seán Connolly and his unit pulled out towards City Hall.

General James Connolly would accompany the headquarters staff of the Irish Volunteers as they marched towards the General Post Office on Sackville Street. Reports had already been received that other Volunteer units were occupying and securing positions throughout the city.

Finally, Commandant Mallin ordered his unit to move out. Margaret Skinnider, a school teacher from Glasgow in Scotland who had taken a week's holiday to participate in the Rising, cycled off ahead of Mallin's column in order to scout the route. Marching across Butt Bridge and into Tara Street, Joe Connolly left the fire station to join the ranks of the Citizen Army. They marched at a brisk pace on towards Grafton Street. The insurrection had commenced, and there was no turning back now.

Chapter 2

Easter Monday 24 April, 1916: Attack on an Empire

At 12.10 hours, Captain Seán Connolly and thirty members of the Irish Citizen Army walked up Cork Hill towards Dublin Castle, the administrative centre of British rule in Ireland. The group divided in two, one section remaining near City Hall while the other marched towards the gates of the Castle.

Constable James O'Brien of the Dublin Metropolitan Police was on duty at the gate, and his colleague Constable Peter Folan was preparing to go home.

When the Citizen Army approached, the constable made a sign to them with his left hand to pass on up Castle Street. The gate was open all the time, as usual. I think it was a man in the first or second line of marchers that raised his gun and shot the policeman. Another took aim and fired at me, but I threw myself to the ground.[4]

Seán Connolly had raised his rifle, squeezed the trigger and shot the policeman dead. Constable James O'Brien was forty-eight years old. He originally came from Kilfergus in County Limerick, and had over twenty-one years of service in the police force.

The British soldier on guard duty attempted to raise his rifle, but decided to retreat back to the guardhouse before firing his weapon. Volunteers Thomas Kane, Christy Brady, George Connolly, Thomas Daly, Philip O'Leary and James Seerey opened fire at the guardhouse and hurled a canister type bomb through the window. Though the incendiary failed to explode it caused confusion amongst the defenders. The sentries did not return fire, and surrendered to the attackers as they had only blank ammunition. These type of rounds had been issued to the guards as no serious military threat had been expected, and also with the thought that the police could deal with any civil disturbance that was likely to arise. The six British soldiers were disarmed and tied up with their own puttees. Connolly's men did not venture further into the Castle complex but took up position in the guardhouse, where they enjoyed a saucepan of stew that the guards had been preparing for themselves. With the guardhouse secured, the rest of Connolly's unit could now occupy City Hall.

As the attack began, three high-ranking British officials were meeting within the walls of the Castle. Sir Matthew Nathan, Under-Secretary for Ireland, Major Ivor Price of Military Intelligence and A.H. Norway, Secretary of the Post Office were discussing a plan to suppress the Irish Volunteers and Citizen Army following a week of incidents that had climaxed in the arrest of Roger Casement and the interception of a consignment of arms by the Royal Navy. Norway had warned Nathan and the Castle authorities of the escalating threat from the Irish Volunteer movement and the possibility of an insurrection. He had urged them to take action, but to no avail.

> ... Nathan had omitted all precautions, making no arrests and leaving the city during that critical weekend denuded so far of troops that when the Castle gates were shut on himself ... there was no force nearer than the Curragh which could be used to restore us to freedom.[5]

On hearing the sound of gunfire, Major Price immediately called out the guard from Ship Street Barracks. Twenty-five soldiers took up defensive positions within the Castle grounds and prepared for an all-out assault on the complex.

Having secured the area, Captain Seán Connolly ordered his main force of ten men and ten women to take up position in City Hall. Connolly knew the building and its layout as he was employed there as a clerk in the motor tax office. Using a specially impressed key to open the main door of the Hall, the armed group immediately began to fortify their position. They proceeded methodically to smash everything. The windows were punched out with rifle butts; china ornaments, pictures and glass cabinets were broken and reduced to pieces. Curtains were ripped down and cushions and carpets were laid over window-sills. Everything that might shatter with a bullet or a piece of shrapnel was broken first, so that it could not be added to the lethal debris that would be hurled around the room once the action started. The soft furnishings were laid over the sills to prevent stone splinters, and armchairs and office furniture were pushed against the walls for added protection and firing rests. It took just a few minutes to transform City Hall into a fortress. Splitting his force in two, Captain Connolly deployed half his men on the ground floor and with the remainder he proceeded onto the roof that circled the huge dome of the hall. He immediately began placing his men in position at various points along the roof and behind its parapet, where his men had a commanding view of the surrounding area. From his vantage point on the roof, fifteen-year-old Matthew Connolly was ordered to take cover behind the stonework of the roof pediment facing down Parliament Street. He was told to watch for any British military personnel that were advancing towards the city. Unarmed, individual soldiers were not to be interfered with.[6]

Nearby, other men from Captain Connolly's detachment took up position. John Byrne, Eddie Connolly, Charlie Darcy, James Donnolly, William Halpin and Sam King occupied the roof of 'Henry and James' outfitters on the corner of Cork Hill and Parliament Street. Frank Fitzpatrick, Martin Kelly, Arthur King and James McDonnell took up position within the Mail and Express offices on Dame Street. Patrick Byrne, Thomas Healy and John O'Keeffe occupied the nearby Synod House. Within the Huguenot graveyard on Nicholas Street, Michael Delaney, William Oman and Patrick Williams took up positions behind the headstones. The rear of the Castle was to be covered by Irish Volunteers under the command of Thomas McDonagh, who had occupied Jacob's biscuit factory on Aungier Street. From these posts, any advance to or from the Castle could be checked.

Initial sorties by both sides failed to establish the numbers of combatants within the environs of the Castle entrance. Both groups began to consolidate their positions. A gun battle erupted between those positioned on the roof of City Hall and the British troops who had occupied the Bermingham Tower in the Castle grounds. Bullets smashed through windows and ricocheted off the stonework.

Dublin Castle was not only the centre for British administration in Ireland, but the complex also housed a Red Cross hospital. As the first shots of the Rising rang out, there were sixty-seven patients being cared for within the building. A British officer entered the ward and alerted the medical personnel that an insurrection was in progress throughout the city and that they were to remain under cover.

Major Price telephoned British Headquarters in Parkgate Street requesting that a relief force be sent immediately to the Castle. Realising that a full-scale insurrection was in progress, Colonel H.V. Cowan, Assistant Adjutant General, telephoned Portobello, Richmond and the Royal Barracks to inform the battalion commanders of events in the city. He requested that all in lying piquets – approximately one hundred armed soldiers kept in a state of readiness – be sent immediately to secure Dublin Castle.

The first objective undertaken by the troops was to recover possession of the Magazine Fort in the Phoenix Park. They were then ordered to relieve the Castle, and to strengthen the guards at the Viceregal Lodge and other points of importance throughout the city. The Magazine was quickly reoccupied, but the insurgents had erected a number of barricades to hinder any relief columns moving to the Castle. Between 13.40 hours and 14.00 hours, one hundred and eighty British soldiers from the 3rd Royal Irish Rifles, the 10th Royal Dublin Fusiliers and the 6th Reserve Cavalry Regiment and a machine-gun detachment from

Portobello Barracks managed to gain entry to the Castle via the Ship Street entrance.

Lieutenant Charles William Grant of the 10th Royal Dublin Fusiliers stationed in the Royal Barracks led a relief force towards the Castle.

I met Colonel Tighe of the Royal Irish Fusiliers making his way to the Royal Barracks. He joined our party, and as senior officer took command. Passing Christchurch Cathedral a few revolver shots were fired. We entered a street running along the sidewalls of the approach to the entrance of the Lower Castle Yard. Here we came under heavy fire from the rebels in City Hall, which resulted in a further twenty wounded. The colonel decided that we should divide the rest of the party. He proceeded with his group down the long steps to the Ship Street entrance to the Castle. I took my group of about ten men round by Ship Street Barracks, where we entered the Castle, having got them to open the gate for us and rejoined the rest of our original party. On entering the Castle we found very few troops in occupation, and to the best of my knowledge we were the only troops in control at that time.[7]

A telephone call was also placed to the Central Army Headquarters of Central Command at the Curragh Camp in County Kildare. An advance guard from the 3rd Reserve Cavalry Brigade was immediately dispatched to Dublin to secure Kingsbridge Railway Station (now Heuston Station). On being briefed of the situation that was unfolding in Dublin, Colonel W.H.M. Lowe ordered the remainder of the Brigade to make ready for entrainment to Dublin.

British troops immediately began taking up vantage points in the Castle in order to establish sniping positions where they could fire at those in City Hall. Sergeant Frederick William Burke of the 10th Royal Dublin Fusiliers scaled a ladder leading onto the Castle roof. Shots rang out, hitting the NCO, his lifeless body falling to the ground. Sergeant Burke had enlisted in Gravesend, England and was twenty-one years old.

Dr Kathleen Lynn arrived at City Hall minutes after the Irish Citizen Army had occupied the building. Taking her medical equipment from the car, she bade farewell to Countess Markievicz, who drove off towards the Green. In order to gain entry to City Hall, Dr Lynn had to climb over the gates. Once inside she reported to Captain Seán Connolly, who ordered her to take up position on the roof. Taking a small medical bag, she climbed the stairs to the roof, where a fierce gun battle was in progress.

Many of the Volunteers were lying flat on the roof, pressed into whatever cover they could find in the valleys and gullies of the roof, or crouching behind the bullet-chipped balustrades. British snipers on the Bermingham tower had identified the roof of City Hall as their main objective. When a target was identified, a rapid volley of rifle fire would be directed at the concealed gunmen, aiming to kill them, or at least force them to take cover. Bullets sliced through the air as each side tried to kill the other.

Within the Castle, Lieutenant Guy Vickery Pinfield of the 8th King's Royal Irish Hussars was ordered to lead an attack with the objective of securing the main gate of the Castle and the guardhouse. The platoon moved towards the gate under heavy fire, when Captain Pinfield was shot and mortally wounded. A section moved forward and started laying down some strong covering fire, and a group of them managed to pull the dead officer into cover. Francis Sheehy-Skeffington, a well-known Dublin pacifist, braved the hail of gunfire to bring aid to the stricken officer, but it was too late. Lieutenant Guy Vickery Pinfield was twenty-one years old, and was a former student at Cambridge University. He had received his commission in 1914. The platoon fell back, having suffered one officer killed, one officer wounded and approximately thirty ordinary ranks wounded.

The violent events of the morning had shown Crown forces that the Volunteers positioned in City Hall were determined and sufficiently well armed. In order to consolidate their position, and prepare for the relief of the Castle, the military would first have to clear the insurgents from City Hall and its environs – a task that would prove to be easier said than done.

Chapter 3

Easter Monday 24 April, 1916: Noon

The stillness of the beautiful spring afternoon was shattered with shouts of 'Move, move, move!' as Volunteers moved at the double towards St Stephen's Green Park. Volunteer Peter Jackson produced a key that opened the large gate at the Fusiliers Arch. A section covered the main gate of the park while others fanned out and began ordering people out of the Green. The park was crowded with a cross-section of Irish society enjoying the spring sunshine on the bank holiday Monday. A number of shots were fired, while many people looked on in disbelief at the escalating seriousness of the situation.

Young women with children, courting couples and the elderly were ushered out at gunpoint as the side gates were closed and secured. A young lady who refused to leave became hysterical when the gates were closed, and she found herself on the wrong side of the railings. After exchanging a number of words with the sentries she was ejected from the park. An elderly priest who was leaving the park was asked to give absolution to a number of the garrison. Kneeling on the pavement, the group were blessed before they deployed into the park.

Off-duty soldiers were placed under arrest and moved under guard to a greenhouse. A civilian, Laurence J. Kettle, Chief of the Dublin City Electricity Department, was held at gunpoint on orders from Commandant Mallin. If the insurrection succeeded, Kettle would be needed to secure the co-operation of those in charge of utilities within the city. Kettle's brother Thomas was a serving officer in the British Army.

Curious onlookers crowded around the entrance to the park, trying to get a glimpse of what was happening within the grounds, while others jeered at the rebels.

> A man was standing inside the gates, holding a rifle and looking intently down Grafton Street. Some girls were chaffing him, and asked him if he was not scared to death, and what would his mother say if she could see him now, and was he not afraid that she would give him a beating. But he paid no heed to their chaff, though now and then, when someone obscured his vision of the street, he gruffly ordered them away and, if they did not move speedily, threatened to shoot them, 'G'long with you!' they would say, still chaffing but a little uncertain.[8]

Having entered through the Fusiliers' Arch at the western side of the park, Commandant Mallin established a Forward

Command Post in a park kiosk near the statue of Lord Ardilaun (Sir Arthur Guinness). The dangerous task of carrying despatches was detailed to some of the female section as well as members of the Fianna Éireann. Their job would entail passing through occupied territory in order to deliver messages to General Headquarters at the Post Office in Sackville Street. Shortly after occupying the park, Commandant Mallin sent off his first despatch to Commander James Connolly.

With the evacuation of civilians complete, Captain Christopher Poole allocated a company of men to secure each entrance into the Green. While some gates were barricaded with wheelbarrows, gardening implements and park benches, Captain Poole ordered a number of men to dig slit trenches and foxholes covering the main entrances. The company started 'digging in,' getting out their trenching tools and excavating shallow holes so that they could get below ground level but still have a good firing position. James O'Shea and Jim Fox dug a slit trench inside the railings covering the approach from Dawson Street:

> We dug for a couple of hours and made a nice job of it, putting some bushes around it as camouflage. We made a shelf for bombs and the shotguns by cutting into the earth.[9]

The overhanging foliage of the trees that lined the park perimeter concealed the positions from view. Margaret Ffrench-Mullen established a first aid post at the bandstand while Mary Hyland and Kathleen Cleary set up a field kitchen in the summer-house. In order to identify the makeshift field hospital, a Red Cross flag was hoisted over the post.[10] Other women were detailed to commandeer food from local sources. Lily Kempson held up a bread cart at the point of a revolver, while Mary Hyland held up a milk cart in a similar fashion. Both women then brought their caches into the park. Nellie Gifford carried sacks of bread to be distributed amongst the garrison. It is noteworthy that a significant part of Mallin's unit consisted of women, who in the days to follow would be called upon to prove their worth on many occasions. They had been trained in the use of firearms and first aid, and would find themselves in the front line of battle within hours of taking up their positions.

To the north of the Green, the Shelbourne Hotel dominated the skyline. On Easter Monday 1916 the hotel bar was full of off duty British officers, equestrian types and landed gentry who had travelled to Dublin for the Spring Show and the Fairyhouse Races. Though the occupation of this building was part of the original plan, it had to be abandoned due to Commandant Mallin's meagre force.

Outside the railings of the park an I.C.A. section were detailed to construct a series of roadblocks on the surrounding streets. Vehicles were commandeered at gunpoint, and placed in blocking positions across the road. Those drivers and occupants who failed to comply were shot. The writer James Stephens witnessed the violent death of James Cavanagh as he was gunned down while attempting to retrieve his dray from a barricade.

The man was picked up and carried to a hospital beside the Arts Club. There was a hole in the top of his head, and one does not know how ugly blood can look until it has been seen in clotted hair. As the poor man was being carried in, a woman plumped to her knees in the road and began not to scream but to screech. At that moment the Volunteers were hated.[11]

Having seen the man gunned down, the group of onlookers carried the dead body to the kerb and shouted, 'We'll be back for you, damn you!' Sporadic shooting by the Volunteers inflicted more civilian casualties in the area. While walking through the revolving doors of the Shelbourne Hotel, George Smethwick was shot and seriously wounded. Victor Brooke was hit in the leg as he sat down for lunch in the dining-room, and Mr Armiger had his jaw shattered by a bullet as he sat in the sitting room of the hotel. The manager immediately ordered the doors to be closed and secured as he transferred his guests to the safety of a writing-room at the rear of the building.[12] An eight-year-old girl, Doreen Carphim, was shot and wounded whilst walking past the Unitarian Church. Many of the casualties were non-combatants, and the nearby Mercer's hospital recorded sixteen dead and two hundred and seventy-eight civilians wounded during Easter week. The hospital was overwhelmed, and temporary casualty clearing stations had to be provided at premises on Merrion Square and Harcourt Street.

On arrival at the Green, Countess Markievicz reported to Commandant Mallin. Due to the fact that his force was seriously under strength, and that he needed every combatant who could handle a weapon, he decided to assign the Countess to the Green garrison. She immediately set off to inspect its defences, and at the Harcourt Street entrance the Vice Commandant encountered a group of Volunteers who were arguing with a member of the Dublin Metropolitan Police who refused to leave his post. As the police officer berated the Volunteers for their occupation of the park, Markievicz drew her automatic pistol and aimed it at the policeman. Other Volunteers raised their rifles, and without warning three shots rang out in quick succession, hitting the constable. Onlookers carried the wounded police officer to the Meath Hospital, where he died shortly after admission. Constable Michael Lahiff was twenty-eight years old and had five years of service in the force.

Nearby, Captain Richard McCormack led an Irish Citizen Army section towards Harcourt Street Railway terminus, one of the Green's outposts. As they approached Harcourt Street, the unit sighted a young British officer on horseback accompanied by his orderly, also on horseback. Tension mounted as the distance between the two groups narrowed and Volunteers released the safety catches of their weapons. McCormack ordered his men to remain calm, as any shooting at this early stage could jeopardise their mission and alert the authorities. As both groups drew abreast, Captain McCormack saluted the surprised British officer, who instinctively returned the salute. The pace quickened as the Irish Citizen Army group continued towards their destination. Glancing back, Captain McCormack saw the officer and his orderly gazing after the column suspiciously.

On reaching the terminus, Captain Richard McCormick ordered his men to seize the railway terminal building. Day-trippers panicked as armed men rushed the building. Groups of men attempted to evade capture by taking refuge inside the ticket office. The door was burst open and they were marched out under guard. Others sought escape by any means possible, as Frank Robbins recalled:

A uniformed staff officer of the British Army, obviously on holiday, looked out from the restaurant. My first impulse was to shoot. But seeing no visible side-arms I called on him to surrender. He very foolishly ran behind the door, banging it shut. The upper portion of the door was smoked glass. This helped to save his life, for on reaching the door I kicked it open, called on him to surrender, while at the same time watching his figure as he flattened himself against the wall behind the door. He had no fight left. When he surrendered I handed him over to Captain McCormack.[13]

While McCormack's men took up position in the station, Lieutenant M. Kelly secured the railway bridge over the Grand Canal, and Captain John O'Neill took up position on the railway bridge overlooking the South Circular Road. In order to prevent any cavalry advancing on their position, McCormack ordered the construction of a barricade outside the train station. As his men moved a number of automobiles and carts to form the obstruction, a tram shuttled into view. The men decided to commandeer the vehicle for their barricade. The driver, however, had other ideas.

The driver proved to be an enterprising chap. He whipped off the control handle of the tram and changed to the other end, while the conductor reversed the trolley. It was the quickest bit of work on the part of two tramway employees I had ever seen. Detecting their intention, I as the officer in charge gave the order to fire. We planned to frighten the tram crew, but not to kill, and our widely aimed volley had no effect whatsoever. The driver and his mate were not to be frightened, and undauntedly stuck to their post and drove the tram out of danger. We were furious at the loss of our potential barricade, but we could not but admire the crew's adroit manoeuvre and their coolness in danger.[14]

A second group of Volunteers, consisting of seven men under the command of Joe Daly, had broken away from Captain McCormack's unit and were proceeding towards Portobello. They had been ordered to occupy and hold Davy's public house on the corner of Richmond Street and Charlemont Mall. These premises covered Portobello Bridge and the nearby military barracks in Rathmines. As the Volunteers marched towards their objective, the two mounted cavalrymen became suspicious and began shadowing the group.

The Volunteers quickened their pace, and rushed to get ahead of the mounted troopers. This action resulted in the Cavalry officer preparing to charge the Volunteers. Daly ordered his men to fix bayonets and spread out on the road and prepare to receive a mounted attack. With discipline and military precision, the men took up position to receive the attack. The officer spurred his mount towards the Irish formation. A shot rang out, narrowly missing the cavalryman, who reined in his horse, turned sharply and galloped away.

Davy's Public house stood at the corner of Charlemont Street and Richmond Street South, adjacent to the Grand Canal. As they reached the building, Volunteer James Joyce, an employee of the licensed premises, kicked open the door. As the men poured into the building, the proprietor Davy stood behind the bar. On seeing the Volunteers occupy his pub, Davy roared, 'I'm giving you a week's notice, Joyce!' 'And I'm giving you five minutes, Mister Davy!' replied Joyce, raising his rifle and emptying a magazine into the bar.[15] Patrons dived for cover as shards of glass exploded throughout the bar.

Ejecting the proprietor by force, the squad immediately set about fortifying their post. Within minutes a shout came down from upstairs that a platoon of British soldiers from the 3rd (Reserve) Battalion Royal Irish Rifles were making their way towards the bridge from Portobello barracks. Taking up position at the windows, Daly ordered his men to hold their fire until the British were within range. As they came to the bridge, Daly shouted 'Fire, fire, fire!' A fusillade of shots ripped into the British formation, forcing them to scatter and take up firing positions behind the low canal bank wall. There was a strange moment of silence as the firing stopped. Reinforcements were hurriedly despatched from the barracks, along with a Maxim machine-gun that was wheeled up to the bridge on a bogie. Onlookers watched as riflemen took up position along the southern bank of the canal. The first rank lay flat on their stomachs, the second kneeling, and an officer whose tunic had been torn to shreds by bullets in the initial contact walked up and down with his revolver in his hand, scornful yet relieved of the rebels' poor marksmanship.

A barrage of rifle- and machine-gun-fire was unleashed at the upper windows of the building, the bullets leaving pock-marks in the brickwork. A British officer accompanied by a platoon of soldiers charged across the bridge and began smashing the windows and battering the door in an attempt to breach an entry. However, unknown to the British soldiers, Joe Daly and his squad had vacated the building via a rear entrance and were making their way back to the Green.

Having achieved his objectives, and covering the occupation of posts throughout the city, Captain Richard McCormack also withdrew his force from Harcourt Street Railway Terminus. The units made their way through the old exhibition grounds and out through the grounds of University College in Earlsfort Terrace and onto St Stephen's Green. Arriving at the park, the men were immediately detailed with securing the entrance at Earlfort Terrace. They dug in, using the flower-beds that ran parallel with the railings as slit trenches. The spoil was spread around the top of the trench to provide some extra cover.

Morale was high among the men and women of the Irish Citizen Army. Commandant Mallin sent Margaret Skinnider on her bicycle to Headquarters at the General Post Office with a despatch stating that he had secured his objective. She returned some time later with a message from Connolly stating that the city was in rebellion and that all objectives had been secured. A copy of the Proclamation had also been sent to the garrison from the GPO, and it was passed around the men, who read the document in silence.

While a sense of relief spread through the park's garrison, Commandant Mallin was apprehensive, as he knew that it was only the beginning, and that the newly declared republic was far from secure. Only time would tell how insecure it was.

Chapter 4

Easter Monday 24 April, 1916: Afternoon

Captain Kit Poole moved from post to post within the park, ensuring that defensive positions were sufficient to withstand an attack. Barricades were reinforced and fields of fire checked as he spoke to the men.

Since the beginning of their action, an estimated twenty men and women had augmented Commandant Mallin's small garrison. On passing by the Green, Nora O'Daly of the Cumann na mBan had accepted Markievicz's invitation to join the garrison.

Having travelled throughout the country issuing MacNeill's countermanding order, Professor Liam O'Briain, a lecturer in Romance languages at the National University, and his friend Harry Nicholls, an employee of Dublin Corporation, had returned to Dublin to find the Rising in progress. Arriving at the Green, both men stated that they were members of the Irish Volunteers and requested to join the garrison within the park.

Welcoming the men, Lieutenant Bob de Coeur issued them with weapons and ammunition before assigning them to their duties, digging a foxhole covering the Leeson Street entrance to the park.

Commandant Mallin ordered Sergeant Frank Robbins to take a squad and search the Royal College of Surgeons on the western side of the Green. Information had been received that a number of rifles and a quantity of ammunition belonging to the Officer Training Corps of the College were being stored in the building. Built on the site of a former Quaker graveyard, this early-nineteenth-century building with its granite façade was located at the corner of St Stephen's Green and York Street. Its ornate pediment reflected the afternoon sunshine, highlighting the Royal arms and its three statues, Athena (Goddess of wisdom and war), Asclepius (God of medicine) and Hygiea (Goddess of health). Robbins's squad consisted of Fred Ryan, John Joe Hendrick, David O'Leary, Mary Hyland and Lily Kempson. Vice Commandant Markievicz also accompanied the group. As the squad walked out the gate *en route* to the College, Robbins noticed that the caretaker was attempting to usher a man out through the front door so he could secure the entrance. The group walked towards York Street in an attempt to deceive the caretaker into thinking that the College of Surgeons was not their intended target. With only a few yards to go they broke into a run and charged towards the main entrance. The caretaker slammed the door shut as a shot rang out, splintering the top right hand side of the door. This action unnerved the caretaker, who failed to secure the locking bolt home. With the full force of his weight and strength, Robbins crashed through the door and shoved the barrel of his revolver against the throat of the caretaker. Within minutes the building had been secured. Walking through the rooms, Robbins was greeted by the strong surgical smell that permeates halls of medicine. Tagged remains preserved in jars of formaldehyde, surgical implements and what seemed like thousands of medical books filled the building. The caretaker and his family were bundled into a room, where Robbins began interrogating his prisoners in relation to the whereabouts of the weapons, but to no avail. Lily Kempson reported back to Mallin that a preliminary search of the building had revealed nothing. Commandant Mallin ordered Robbins to hold the College of Surgeons as a 'fall back position' in case it was needed. Tables and benches were piled against the doors, and medical books were piled high on the sills of the windows. The side door opening onto York Street was kept clear for egress, but was kept under guard. Making his way onto the roof, Robbins unfurled a tricolour flag and prepared to run it up the flag-pole. He had considerable difficulty in attaching the flag, as the halyard was jammed and would not move. With the assistance of David O'Leary, he managed to hoist the flag to the top of the pole. The flag blew gently in the spring breeze. Robbins established an observation post on the roof and detailed O'Leary and John Joe Hendrick to cover the approaches to the building.

Liam Ó Briain and his colleagues were still digging their foxholes when Bob de Coeur shouted, 'Fall in!' to which Ó Briain replied from the bottom of his hole, 'Fall in? Aren't we in already?' Bob replied, 'Get out so and line up!' Orders had come through that de Coeur was to take a company of men and occupy two houses that overlooked Leeson Street Bridge. As they marched out the gate an old man stopped, removed his hat and bowed his head as if paying respect to a passing religious ceremony, an ominous sign.

At Dublin Castle, the gun battle between insurgents and Crown forces intensified. British snipers ensconced on the Bermingham Tower engaged Irish Volunteers on the roof of City Hall. Bullets impacted into the masonry as soldiers from each side momentarily exposed themselves, trying to manoeuvre into better firing positions. One British soldier, having fired, attempted to roll away from his position, but was immediately hit by several rounds and sprawled lifeless over the battlements of the tower.

Captain Seán Connolly waded through the sea of enemy fire on the roof of City Hall, pointing out potential targets and ordering a rapid fire against British snipers positioned in the Castle tower. As he stood up to move once again, a single shot rang out, killing the young Irish officer. Medic Bridget Dawson crawled to the stricken officer's side, but he was already dead. Captain Seán Connolly lived in Philipsburg Avenue in Sandymount, Dublin. He was thirty-three years old, and was an active member of the Gaelic League and the Gaelic Athletic Association. His brothers Eddie, George, Joe and Matthew and his sister Katie were all involved in the insurrection. Seán Connolly's death left a widow; two sons aged three and a half and two years and a daughter aged eight months. His younger brother Matthew was only a few yards away on the same roof at the time of his death.

By 16.00 hours British reinforcements were pouring into Dublin city. Sixteen hundred dismounted troopers arrived by train from the Curragh Camp to Kingsbridge railway terminus. Captain Carl Elliotson of the 3rd Reserve Cavalry Brigade was detailed to take a unit of men and a machine-gun section from the station to Dublin Castle. A number of hand trolleys were procured in order to carry the machine-guns and boxes of ammunition.

Moving out along the South Quays, Captain Elliotson managed to pass the Guinness Brewery and filter through the side-streets and alley-ways without meeting serious opposition until he eventually reached the Ship Street entrance of Dublin Castle at 17.30 hours. On arrival, Captain Elliotson was ushered into an officers' briefing that brought everyone up to speed with developments within the city. It was imperative to secure the Castle and the surrounding area in order to establish a secure route for reinforcements into the city centre. In securing Dame Street, British forces could then make their way to Trinity College, which was garrisoned by a small number of British troops and Officer Training Corps. To proceed with this plan, however, the rebels ensconced in City Hall would have to be removed.

A reconnaissance of the area would have to be undertaken to locate the surrounding Volunteer positions. Captain Elliotson edged his way down towards the gates of the Castle, keeping close to the walls in order to avoid detection. Having located the Volunteer posts, the officer gauged his lines of fire before retracing his steps and returning to the inner yard. A Vickers machine-gun was assembled on the roof above the office of Augustine Birrell, the Chief Secretary of Ireland. Those in the Red Cross hospital were alerted that a full-scale assault was about to begin. A nurse recalled:

We had been sent a message: all blinds were to be pulled down and all lights turned out, and to be prepared for noise, as machine-guns were going to start. We groped round in pitch darkness, unable to see who was who, so it was hopeless to try and do anything – and then the guns began. Such a noise! It was well that they had warned us.

It was quite unlike any firing I had heard before, and varied from a rifle much as a cinema differs from a photograph. We comforted ourselves with the thought of the last of the rebels' heels, and that in a few moments our seven hours of excitement would be over, and we should return to *status quo ante*; but it was not long before we began to be undeceived.[16]

An attack force was assembled in the upper yard of the Castle. Ammunition and hand-grenades were distributed as they prepared their weapons for the assault. Soldiers took up position and a covering fire was opened up against the City Hall.

At the gate of the Castle, those Volunteers holed up in the guardhouse realised that their position was untenable and that a major assault was imminent. On searching the room, they discovered a doorway leading to a small cell hidden behind a press. Within the cell there was a side door that opened onto Castle Street. This escape route enabled them to vacate the building unseen. Taking their weapons, they crept silently from the building and made their way through Castle Street to Lahiff's shop on the same side of the street as the guardroom. Fearing capture, Tom Kane, who had been entrusted with the membership roll of the Irish Citizen Army, hid it in a chimney of the building.

The death of Captain Seán Connolly had left the small City Hall garrison in the hands of John J. O'Reilly and Dr Kathleen Lynn. Both officers realised that their position was vulnerable. Helena Molony was sent to headquarters at the General Post Office to ask for reinforcements for City Hall. She was told that men were scarce and that the only thing to do was to 'hang on'.

She returned to the Hall and reported the situation to O'Reilly and Dr Lynn. Outnumbered and outgunned, the officers knew the coming fight would be short and sharp.

British sniper fire was now being directed at all Irish Citizen Army positions. Volunteer Charles Darcy was shot and killed on the roof of Henry and James. He was fifteen years old.

Later that afternoon, in response to the garrison's request for reinforcements, James Connolly despatched Volunteer George Norgrove with a force of seven men to the City Hall. On entering the building they immediately took up firing positions. The small garrison that held City Hall and its outposts now numbered fifty men and women. Preparing to attack these posts were over four hundred trained British soldiers. The odds were beginning to weigh heavily against republican forces.

Chapter 5

Easter Monday 24 April, 1916: Evening

At 17.00 hours British forces launched their assault on the City Hall. Rifles and machine-guns all combined to create an overwhelming cacophony of noise as every weapon opened up at once at the Volunteer positions.

Bullets sliced through the windows of City Hall, sending clouds of plaster dust into the air as sections of cornice and wall disintegrated under the onslaught. On the roof, sixteen-year-old Annie Norgrove was engulfed in a cloud of brick dust as bullets ricocheted above her head as she attempted to bring water to the parched Volunteers. On her hands and knees she crawled along the roof parapet as chimney-pots exploded above her, showering her with debris.

At the upper yard of the Castle, British soldiers drawn from a number of regiments formed a storming party. This composite unit moved forward, waiting for the order to attack.

On the blast of a whistle one hundred soldiers charged forward and secured the Provost Marshal's building. They were unable to penetrate further due to the number of internal barricades and obstacles that had been erected by the insurgents. Close quarter gun battles erupted between the British soldiers and the Irish Volunteers. Another wave of British troops charged forward and were beaten back by intense gunfire. A third unit armed with hand-grenades was despatched, but this time they were sent through the Castle cellars, emerging on the far side of the Hall. Appearing under the windows of the City Hall, these soldiers fired at point-blank range into the building. However, their position was exposed to the rifle fire from the Volunteers on the roof and they suffered a number of casualties. The machine-gunner traversed his weapon and sprayed the roof with bullets killing the garrison's second in command, John J. O'Reilly. A resident of Gardiner Street, O'Reilly was twenty-eight years old.

Dr Katheleen Lynn recalled 'the bullets falling like hail' on the windows of City Hall.[17] This suppressive fire enabled the British troops to breach an entry into the Hall. Storming the building, British troops opened fire into the darkness. Gunfire echoed throughout the building and Louis Byrne, one of the Irish Citizen Army reinforcements, was shot and killed. He was forty-six years old and a resident of Summerhill in Dublin.

Under the onslaught, the Volunteer garrison fell back, many of them retreating to the upper floors, shooting as they went. Dr Lynn remained on the ground floor caring for the wounded amidst a hail of gunfire, smoke and debris. A British officer, gun in hand, advanced through the dust and shouted, 'Anyone here? Speak or I shoot!' Dr Lynn stepped forward and stated her rank and that there were a number of wounded being cared for in the area. Surrendering her force, Dr Lynn asked for the wounded to be evacuated. Stretcher-bearers carried Thomas Coyle and John Finlay to the Red Cross hospital within the Castle grounds. Within the labyrinth of City Hall, British soldiers commenced room-clearing operations. In an upper room, a British officer who assumed that she was a civilian caught up in the attack discovered Jenny Shanahan, a member of the garrison. She stated that there were over one hundred armed men on the roof of the building. This delayed the British advance considerably, and it was only when the officer brought his charge to Ship Street Barracks, where the other prisoners welcomed her, that he realised he had been tricked. He exclaimed, 'Oh, so you are one of them, are you?' and promptly handed her over to her comrades.

After a brief respite, the military prepared to assault the upper floors. Dashing up the stairs to the upper rooms, the soldiers were met by a hail of gunfire. Confined in such a small area, the advantage of numbers and firepower was lost as Irish and British forces clashed and a hand-to-hand struggle ensued. Overpowering the defenders on the upper floors, British troops pressed home their attack. Bursting out onto the roof, the soldiers opened fire into the last of the defenders, killing George Geoghegan. A native of County Kildare, Geoghegan was thirty-six years old and was employed as a warehouse packer. His death left a widow and three children.

City Hall had fallen. One Volunteer, William Halpin, attempted to evade capture by hiding in a chimney, but was discovered covered from head to toe in soot. He was taken into custody by the military and escorted into the Castle.

It was vital to identify the Volunteer positions around the Castle, and in order to garner intelligence, Lieutenant Charles William Grant of the 10th Royal Dublin Fusiliers was ordered to lead a reconnaissance unit towards St Stephen's Green and its surrounds. At 19.00 hours, the Recce patrol exited the Castle through the rear gate and made their way towards Aungier Street.

Near Jacob's factory the party was recognised and the question arose as to how to get back to the Castle. In front of St Matthias Church I saw a number of men in military formation, and I went back down Harcourt St., and in front of the children's hospital I noticed a number of rifles in the windows of the upstairs apartments. I was turning over in my mind as to the safest route to take, when suddenly a man walked out from the hall of a tenement house near Montague Street where we had halted. I covered him with my revolver, got all the information I could get out of him, and realising that this was his neighbourhood, asked him if he could guide us back to Dublin Castle. He agreed to do this, and as I knew the streets around well, took him and told him if we were attacked we would shoot him immediately. I placed him in charge of Sergeant Robinson, my platoon sergeant, whom I knew would not hesitate in acting should anything untoward arise. Our prisoner was shaking with fright, and could as a result scarcely speak. I knew in a general way how to get back to the Castle, and warned him with a revolver in my hand that any move to give us away would be devastation for him. He brought us back through alleys, which I was not aware of, and guided us to the back gate of the Castle. I had not much money on me, but I gave it all to him, and told him not to mention the guidance that he had given to anyone.[18]

On returning to the Castle he informed his superiors that rebel forces held many of the surrounding streets.

The British now turned their attention to the surrounding insurgent positions. A large crowd of onlookers had gathered at the top of Lord Edward Street, while others had moved down nearer the Castle entrance. Crouching in doorways or huddled against the walls of buildings, the civilians were not aware of the dangers that were about to be unleashed.

Second Lieutenant F. O'Neill and a platoon from the 5th Royal Dublin Fusiliers were given the objective of capturing the *Daily Express* offices and the Henry and James store across from City Hall. Suppressive machine-gun fire raked the frontage of the buildings, sending clouds of red brick dust rising into the air. After fifteen minutes of fire, the platoon fixed bayonets and charged out the Castle gates. The Irish Citizen Army contingent opened fire, forcing the British to fall back. A sudden lull in the firing saw stretcher-bearers rushing forward to take the dead and wounded from the field of battle.

The machine-gun opened up again, a withering hail of bullets hitting the building. A second wave of soldiers rushed from the Castle gates, but this time the machine-gun kept up its relentless chatter as they dashed across the thirty yards of open ground towards their objective. Men fell as the fire emitting from the Mail Offices hit them. On reaching the wall of the building, British soldiers lobbed grenades through the windows. On successfully breaching an entry, soldiers poured into the building but discovered that the small garrison had escaped over the roofs of the adjacent buildings and had reached the relative safety of Essex Street. Stretcher-bearers once again made their way out from the Castle gates and collected the dead and wounded, returning to the Red Cross hospital.

Within the Exchange Hotel on Parliament Street, a group from the Hibernian Rifles took up position.

Commander James Connolly had sent this small force from the GPO in support of the City Hall garrison. Having occupied the hotel, British forces launched an attack and were beaten back after a hectic gun battle. Volunteer John Joseph Scallon recalls:

> ... units of the Irish Fusiliers and the Inniskilling Fusiliers advanced to storm our position and were met by a fusillade from our shotgun men and rifles. They were actually slaughtered by our fire – 23/4 of them killed or wounded. I was on a roof near a chimney when a bullet caught Edward Walsh, one of our men, and literally tore his stomach out. He died that evening.[19]

Edward Walsh was a member of the Hibernian Rifles, and was forty-three years old. His death left a widow and two children.

With many of the ICA posts now under British control, those Volunteers who had evaded capture dispersed or tried to link up with other units. Volunteer William Oman made his way home. He changed out of his uniform before making his way to the College of Surgeons, where he rejoined the Volunteers.

After hours of fighting, British troops had secured the Castle and the immediate area. They had suffered a considerable amount of casualties that now filled the Red Cross hospital.

Prisoners were escorted into the Castle grounds, where they were searched and held under guard. Dr Lynn and the other women were separated from the male prisoners and held in Ship Street Barracks. She recalls:

> We slept on what they called biscuits. They were not biscuits. They were like little mattresses in sections, about three of which would be long enough to lie on. We had dusty, grey blankets, which were all crawling with lice. I never slept during the time I was there; I could not. The scratching was not so bad during the daytime, but in the night-time it was perfectly awful.[20]

At 22.00 hours Lieutenant Charles William Grant was summoned to the operations room within the Castle. Information had been received that insurgents were positioned within St Stephen's Green Park. This information would have to be verified, and it was suggested that a small force make their way to the Shelbourne Hotel, secure the location, investigate and report back. A platoon from the 10th Royal Dublin Fusiliers were mustered and ordered to make ready to move out towards the hotel. Lieutenant Grant's knowledge of the city enabled the force to reach its destination undetected. On arriving at the hotel Lieutenant Grant immediately began to clear and secure the building as ordered:

> With the aid of the manager I entered every bedroom facing the front and had an embarrassing job, first to request the occupants to leave the room, and if they did not willingly comply with my request, to get them out by

force if necessary. Being a Bank Holiday, and many visitors having returned from the Curragh Races, needless to say that in carrying out my job, I came across visitors who were keen on preserving their identity. In doing so there were many who thought it well to quietly comply with my orders. At the same time I directed the members of my party to barricade the entrances to the hotel with heavy furniture. My orders having been carried out, I returned alone to the Castle, leaving the men to guard the hotel. I slipped out of the side door into Kildare Street, where I occupied the attention of snipers. I ran down Kildare Street like a hare and into Molesworth Lane and into Molesworth Street as a number of rebels were marching along Dawson Street. I got into cover under the front outside the wall of the Diocesan School and lay on my tummy for about twenty minutes until the rebels had passed, after which I proceeded back to the Castle without interruption.[21]

On his return to the Castle, Lieutenant Grant submitted his 'sit rep' (situation report) to Major Ivor Price of Military Intelligence, who decided that the Green could pose a serious threat to any plan to retake the city.

In order to prevent an attack on the Castle, or on Crown forces retaking the city, a detachment would be sent to occupy the Shelbourne Hotel and contain enemy forces in the area. Major Price knew that any failure to contain Volunteer forces in the area could result in a breakout and possible further assaults on the Castle. A desperate but vital mission lay ahead.

Chapter 6

Easter Monday 24 April, 1916: Midnight is a Place

Captain Carl Elliotson of the 3rd Reserve Cavalry Brigade was summoned to the operations room in the Castle and was ordered to 'have a go' at the rebels who were occupying St Stephen's Green. Leaving the briefing, Captain Elliotson immediately began to assemble his force. Within minutes, one hundred and twenty troopers of the 3rd Reserve Cavalry Brigade had amassed in the Castle yard and were preparing to move out towards the Shelbourne Hotel. A .303 Vickers machine-gun was disassembled and placed on two stretchers, enabling the weapon to be carried with ease. A water-cooled, belt-fed weapon, the gun had the capability of firing 450 to 600 rounds per minute. Weighing in at 30lb, its tripod weighed another 50lb.

Thousand round boxes of ammunition weighing 22lb each were distributed between every two men. The gunners carried the spare gun parts. A Lewis machine-gun also made up part of the column's armaments. This squad automatic weapon was fed from a drum magazine that held forty-seven rounds. Operated by a two-man team, the gun was a lightweight, air-cooled weapon that had a cyclic rate of fire of 550 rounds per minute. Extra panniers of ammunition for the weapon were distributed amongst the men. The heavily laden group would have to make their way through enemy-held territory in order to get to their objective: the Shelbourne Hotel. Lieutenant Grant, who possessed a good knowledge of the streets of the city, was detailed to be the 'point man' for the group. Locked and loaded, the assault force moved out of the Castle grounds through the lower gate and into Dame Lane. The platoon moved slowly, cutting through backstreets and alley-ways and running across open streets and junctions. In order to keep the noise to a minimum they were under orders that there was to be no talking. To the men, however, the sound of their rattling kits and hobnailed boots on the pavements sounded like an express train. Arriving in Kildare Street, the column halted fifty yards from the side door of the hotel. The street was illuminated by two electric standards that threatened to reveal the advancing troops. One trooper dashed across the street and managed to open the door. The rest of the party then followed, covering the fifty yards in 'even time' by half sections, managing to evade the sentries that the Irish Citizen Army had posted in the park.

On reaching the building, Captain Elliotson reinforced the ground floor and ensured the barricades were sufficient to withstand an all-out assault. Two men were posted to each window in order to cover the approach from the front and sides of the building. The Vickers machine-gun was carried to the fourth floor and assembled, its field of fire 'zeroed in' onto the Green. The gunners checked their sight lines over the street below. Lieutenant Grant inspected the positions, stating that the blast on a whistle would be the signal to open fire. Captain Elliotson synchronised his watch and ordered his corporal to take thirty men and the squad automatic weapon, the Lewis machine-gun, and make their way to the United Service Club, located a few doors down from the Hotel. Zero hour was set for 04.00 hours.

Each soldier carried an extra pannier of ammunition for the Lewis gun as well as his own kit. Leaving the hotel via the side entrance, the small group moved at the double and managed to cover the distance without being discovered. Staggering into the building, the platoon took stock of their position. They were only a few feet from the Volunteer positions in the Green, and were also within a short distance from Grafton Street. With its elevated entrance staircase and massive bow windows, this private members' club was an imposing building. The soldiers fortified the ground floor and took up firing positions on the upper levels. The Lewis gun was set up and fields of fire were determined.

From their vantage point on the upper floors of the building that they had occupied, the soldiers could see, through the overhanging foliage of the trees, the camp-fires of the Irish Citizen Army. Raised voices could be heard coming from the park. Here and there the glow of a cigarette lit up the darkness as it was inhaled. A clear view was not possible due to the vegetation, but the soldiers knew that their enemy was only a few feet away.

A slight drizzle of rain began to fall as the men in the park settled in for the night. Sentries had been posted at all the approach routes to the Green, and Captain Poole issued passwords to each post. Food had been distributed earlier in the evening, and much of the talk related to the Rising and how it was progressing throughout the country. Men sat around the camp-fires cleaning and oiling their weapons. Those on sentry duty reported that a number of armed men were seen in the vicinity of the Green. On investigation these groups turned out to be Irish Volunteers making their way towards the centre of the city.[22]

From his concealed position facing Dawson Street, Volunteer James O'Shea caught sight of a soldier who came along the pathway outside the railings of the park. O'Shea challenged the soldier and ordered him to halt, believing that his presence so near his post was a possible reconnoitring of their position. The soldier pretended to be drunk, and directed a steady stream of abuse at the men in the trench. Believing the soldier to be a spy, O'Shea raised his shotgun and opened fire. The soldier was flung backwards as the shotgun blast impacted, killing him outright. Two passers-by were ordered to lift the body of the soldier and remove it from the street. When they protested, O'Shea threatened them with the same if they refused. Soon after this incident Commandant Mallin arrived at their position and enquired to whether O'Shea had shot a British soldier. This was confirmed, and O'Shea mentioned that he believed the soldier was checking their position. Mallin left and resumed inspection of all the posts before nightfall and ensured that his position was secure. The men settled down for the night, cradling their weapons in the shelter of a foxhole or a hedge, and tried to grab whatever sleep they could.

On the fourth floor of the Shelbourne hotel, the machine-gunner stood behind his Vickers machine-gun, calmly examining the weapon. He checked the gun, the tripod, the breach cover, the belt, the alignment of the ammunition boxes and the condenser can. Everything was as it should be. His 'loader' tugged at the belt to make sure the feed was working. Traversing the weapon, they had an excellent field of fire into the park. The British soldiers settled into their positions for the remainder of the night. It would be a tense few hours before dawn.

Chapter 7

Tuesday 25 April, 1916: Dawn Attack

At 04.00 hours the shrill blast of a whistle sounded throughout the hotel as the Vickers machine-gunner curled his fingers around the grips, his thumbs resting lightly on the firing button. Pressing the firing plate down, he opened fire in long bursts, traversing the weapon slowly from left to right and back again. Within seconds the bullet belt had been drawn into the weapon, each round pulled out and loaded into the breach then fired, the brass shell ejecting out of the bottom, accumulating in a pile of empty casings on the floor. Simultaneously, a barrage of rifle fire erupted from the windows of the hotel. There were shouts and screams, and the flash of gunfire from behind the screen of trees that lined the perimeter of the park. The Irish Citizen Army was out in the open, and pinned down by soldiers who now had every battlefield advantage.

Within the park, the first indication of the presence of British troops was the burst of machine-gun fire that ripped through the overhanging trees and thudded into the ground. Taken by surprise, the call 'Stand to!' was shouted throughout the park. Men and women grabbed their weapons as bullets whizzed through the air while they sought whatever cover was to hand. Men threw themselves onto the ground in the firing position, making their bodies as small a target as possible. A ragged fire was opened up on the hotel, but all this seemed to do was attract the attention of the machine-gunner, who swivelled his weapon to where the firing had come from. James Corcoran was one of the first to be shot and killed as a blaze of gunfire cut through the trees. Originally from Gorey in County Wexford, Corcoran was thirty-three years old and married with three children.

Outside the railings of the park, three volunteers were caught in the open as they attempted to reinforce the barricade that stretched across the road. A burst of machine-gun fire cut through the group, sending them running for cover. Volunteer Philip Clarke was directly hit, and collapsed on the roadway in full view of the British positions. Bursts of machine-gun fire from the upper windows of the hotel kicked up sparks beside the fallen Volunteer.

On hearing the sound of gunfire, Commandant Mallin had rushed from his Command Post to the Dawson Street entrance, where he witnessed Volunteer Philip Clarke being hit. With no regard for his own safety, Commandant Mallin dashed out the gate towards the stricken Volunteer. Bullets ricocheted off the roadway as Mallin carried Clarke into cover within the park. However, a medic confirmed that the man was already dead. Philip Clarke was a native of Slane in County Meath, and was forty years old. His death left a widow and eight children.

The British garrison within the United Services Club also raked the Green with rifle and machine-gun fire. Bullets sliced through the trees, kicking up sods of clay as they impacted near to Volunteer posts along the northern perimeter of the Green. Men dashed for cover, and others flung themselves to the ground while .303 rounds flew over their heads. The bushes and shrubs on the embankment fronting the Lord Ardilaun statue shielded the Volunteers' command post from view. Mallin ordered his unit to set up a defensive position around the embankment, securing a side entrance as a possible escape route. A group of Volunteers was designated as a 'fire team', and were ordered to lay down a suppressing fire against the United Services Club. This 'fire team' managed to return fire at the gun flashes that were emanating from the windows of the club. In the ensuing gun battle, Volunteer John Francis Adam of Cork Street Dublin was shot dead. His death left a widow and a three-year-old child.

The intensity of the machine-gun fire pinned down many of the men in the park, leaving them with a feeling that they were in a death-trap. All they could do was lie still under the rain of fire. Those who broke cover faced certain death. Under a hail of gunfire, James Fox ran from cover in order to try and get out of the line of fire. The author Max Caulfield writes:

> Hit several times, he fell back, arms spread out, and his agonized screams filled the air. Then, abruptly, he stopped yelling. He still lived, however, for Buttner saw him crawl

a few inches; a movement which brought the wrath of the military down on him again. A second swathe of bullets cut across him and he stopped moving. But each time the machine-gun swept the green lawns bullets struck the body, making it twitch and jerk for a moment as though it were still alive. Another stream of bullets would immediately be directed at the body, each new bullet that hit creating a fresh illusion that the boy still lived. The dead, it seemed, would not be allowed to die.[23]

James Fox, a native of County Meath, was sixteen years old, and was employed as a shop assistant.

Under intense fire, Commandant Mallin realised that his position was untenable and that he had to extricate his force from the Park. He ordered Captain Poole to make ready for the immediate withdrawal of the Irish Citizen Army and to fall back to the College of Surgeons. Word was spread from unit to unit that the blast on a whistle would signal the order to fall back. Each section was to make their way to the Lord Ardilaun statue on the western side of the Green, where there were good natural defences in the form of trees, shrubberies and mounds of earth. They were then to withdraw to the Royal College of Surgeons.

A little after that and from time to time, I heard Commandant Mallin's whistle going, so I prepared to vacate the trench. I had a hard time moving from tree to tree, as every time I moved the tree got a couple of bullets, so I knew that the men on the other side understood their business. My worst time was crossing the bridge in the Park. When I got to the centre of the bridge a bullet struck the parapet and broke a big piece of stone that nearly got me. I ran on towards the summer-house and was then directed to the flower border. I threw myself down and took cover. Madame Markievicz, who with a number of others was taking cover at this spot, told me we were to evacuate the 'the Green' and go to the College of Surgeons. I had to wait nearly an hour, as men were moving in groups to the College and everything was being done in very orderly fashion.[24]

Reacting on instinct and adrenalin, James O'Shea, Paddy Buttner and a number of Volunteers ducked and dived across the open ground of the park as they made their way towards the shrubbery. Bits of raised ground and the scattered vegetation gave them minimal cover.

Word was also sent via Margaret Skinnider that the Volunteer contingent covering Leeson Street bridge was to fall back in sections to the Green, and then to the College of Surgeons.

The Irish Citizen Army unit holding the northern approach to the Green had spent a tense few hours under heavy fire from inside the Shelbourne Hotel. As the men received the order to fall back, bullets snapped through the air and ploughed up explosions of clay as they impacted into the earth. In order to get to the rallying point, many of the men had to crawl, keeping low on their elbows and toes, the hail of bullets seeming intense and impenetrable. Taking up firing positions behind the shrubbery, the Volunteers returned fire in order to provide additional cover for those trying to fall back.

There were a number of wounded who were unable to make it back to the makeshift Red Cross post for attention. Pinned down by the gunfire, many lay bleeding and in great pain.

Moving from post to post, members of the Cumann na mBan risked death in order to bring medical assistance to the wounded. The medics applied field dressings to the wounds and attempted to take the wounded out of the battle zone. The Red Cross flag on the makeshift hospital proved an easy target for the machine-gunner, who emptied belt after belt into the bandstand. Food and medical supplies were abandoned as the medical staff and the wounded vacated the building and ran for cover towards the gatekeeper's lodge. As they gained entry to the lodge, bullets chipped the stonework outside. They collapsed onto the floor, gasping for breath and wondering how they could extricate themselves from their predicament.

As the attack on the Green was taking place, Brigadier General W.H.M. Lowe, commanding the Reserve Cavalry Brigade from the Curragh, arrived with the remainder of his Brigade in Kingsbridge Station (now Heuston Station). Accompanying him were one thousand troops of the 25th Irish Infantry Brigade. Brigadier General Lowe took immediate command of the situation in the absence of the Commander-in-Chief, Major General C.B. Friend, who was on holidays. Having received a situation report stating that the Castle had been secured, Brigadier General Lowe ordered Colonel Portal to establish a line of posts from Kingsbridge Station to Trinity College via the Castle. This course of action would divide the positions of the Irish Volunteers, north and south of the River Liffey, enabling Crown forces to establish a safe line of advance and of communication. The military could then extend operations to the north and south of the city, concentrating on the main rebel strongholds. Intelligence reports revealed that the General Headquarters of the rebel forces was located in the

General Post Office on Sackville Street. General Lowe's strategy involved the destruction of this position, while other rebel posts were to be contained and kept under observation.

On successfully reaching the rallying point at the Lord Ardilaun statue, each Volunteer unit prepared to evacuate the park. The road fronting the College was swept by machine-gun fire from the United Services Club. Captain Poole timed the rate of fire of the machine-gunner ensconced in the United Services Club.

The plan was that, as the gunner prepared to change his spent magazine, the Volunteers would run across the road to the side door of the College on York Street. Each unit would only have a few seconds to cover the distance of over one hundred yards of open ground. The order to 'Make ready!' was shouted down the line as the men edged nearer to the gate.

Chapter 8

Tuesday 25 April, 1916: Fallback

By 08.00 hours, Commandant Mallin was ready to put his exit strategy into practice as the first units of the Irish Citizen Army were in position to evacuate the park. From his vantage point on the roof of the College of Surgeons, Sergeant Robbins and his squad had watched the scenario unfold below his position. Knowing that he had to provide covering fire for his comrades, Robbins ordered his squad to make ready to lay down a covering fire against the United Service Club. Firing at will, the squad began sniping at the puffs of smoke that were emitting from the windows of the United Services Club, and within minutes they silenced a number of the guns within the building as their bullets found their mark.

The machine-gunner ceased firing in order to change his magazine. At the park entrance Captain Poole mustered the men,

Michael Mallin in British
Army uniform India c.1899
(Kilmainham Gaol)

Countess Markievicz, Theo
Fitzgerald, Thomas
McDonald and dog, 1917
Waterford (Kilmainham Gaol)

Brigid Davis, City Hall 1916
(Henry Fairbrother)

Captain Seán Connolly.
Killed in action at City Hall
(Kilmainham Gaol)

British army officers Dublin 1916 (Author's Collection)

British position at the United Services Club (Military Archives)

City Hall (Military Archives)

College Hall, Royal College of Surgeons 1916
(Reproduced courtesy of RCSI)

Commandant Michael Mallin
(Kilmainham Gaol)

Countess Markievicz
(Kilmainham Gaol)

Live bombs on a table in the Royal College of Surgeons 1916
(Reproduced courtesy of RCSI)

Lord Ardilaun's Statue across from the Royal College of
Surgeons (Author's Collection)

The Bridge in St. Stephen's Green (Author's Collection)

The *Evening Mail* offices and Mssrs. Henry & James.
Both buildings occupied by I.C.A. (Military Archives)

The Exchange Hotel on Parliament St. (Military Archives)

Torn portrait of Queen Victoria in Board Room of Royal College of Surgeons 1916 (Reproduced Courtesy of RCSI)

The Royal College of Surgeons and adjoining buildings. These buildings were tunnelled through (Military Archives)

York St. at the side of the Royal College of Surgeons
(Military Archives)

The Gates of Dublin Castle (Military Archives)

Trench from *Daily Sketch* (James Langton)

View from the roof of the Royal College of Surgeons towards
Harcourt St. (Military Archives)

and in separate sections they put their heads down and ran out the west gate towards the College. Within seconds, gunfire erupted and bullets were whistling past the running figures. They made for the side door of the College in York Street. As they reached the door and looked back, one of their number lay in the roadway. The Volunteer in the roadway lay still as the machine-gunner traversed his weapon, spraying the front of the College building. The volunteer feigning death waited till the gunner had expended his magazine and was reloading. As the firing stopped, he jumped to his feet and sprinted the rest of the way, arriving at the College uninjured.

Nearby, three Volunteers: Captain McCormack, Lieutenant Michael Kelly and Michael Donnelly entered number 113 St Stephen's Green, the residence of Donnelly. They shouted across to Robbins on the roof of the College that the British had occupied buildings north of the Green and were launching an attack.

They gestured to Robbins that they were coming down from the roof to join the Volunteers in the College of Surgeons. The three men moved out from the building by a rear laneway, and headed towards the side entrance of the College. As they approached the building they were accosted by a group of men and separation women, armed with iron bars and a hatchet, who launched a vicious attack against the Volunteers. The separation women, whose husbands were serving with the British Army, were the most vicious. Captain McCormack received a wound to the head and blood ran down his face as he stumbled towards the doorway. Sergeant Robbins rushed out and prepared to fire on the hostile mob. He dropped to one knee and was about to pull the trigger when Lieutenant Kelly shouted, 'Frank, don't shoot!'

As Sergeant Robbins hesitated, Lieutenant Kelly grasped his arm and prevented him from firing. The Volunteers retired inside the building, where McCormack's head wound was bandaged.

At the rear of the College a laneway ran alongside the premises of the Direct Trading Mineral Water Co.

The garrison within the building heard a loud knocking on the back gate leading into the laneway. Captain Poole ordered the wicket gate to be covered as it was opened. To the surprise of those in the College, Lieutenants O'Riordan and Seamus Kavanagh of the Irish Volunteers had been sent by Commandant MacDonagh, commander of the Jacob's garrison, in response to an urgent request for reinforcements.

Within the Shelbourne Hotel and the United Services Club, the din from the machine-guns was deafening. The British soldiers manning the windows kept up a rapid rate of fire against the defenders in the Green. Cartridge cases littered the floor, and the smell of cordite wafted through the rooms and hallways.

The machine-gunner traversed his weapon from the Green to the College. Bullets ricocheted off the stonework of the College façade as the Volunteers careered across the roadway. Each section ran the gauntlet of fire, trying to duck and weave the steady stream of fire that was being directed at them. Coming under heavy fire from the roof of the College, the machine-gunner switched his line of fire and emptied a magazine towards the pediment of the building.

A blast of machine-gun fire hit Volunteer Michael O'Doherty, who collapsed, his body hanging over the parapet. Blood flowed down the pediment, staining the stonework. Volunteer David O'Leary rushed forward and grabbing the wounded man's webbing straps, hauled him off the ledge and into cover.

Joe Connolly brought the wounded man down to the lower level of the College and placed him on a stretcher. Though he had caught the full blast of fire, he was still breathing. As he clung to life, O'Doherty was evacuated under fire to the Mercer hospital where he was treated for his wounds.

The small Cumann na mBan unit that had sought shelter in the Gatekeeper's Lodge received the command to fall back to the College of Surgeons. Christine Caffrey led the way, and as they approached the College a hostile crowd attempted to attack the group. Caffrey drew a revolver, and that was enough for the crowd to back down and let the group through to the College.

From the west gate, Commandant Mallin directed his men through the storm of enemy fire. As James O'Shea arrived at the gate, Mallin asked if his entire unit had gone through to the College. When he was answered in the affirmative he ordered the rearguard to make ready to pull out. Mallin stood with his automatic in his hand, and ordered the final group to make a run for it towards the College. Covering fire erupted from the roof of the College as the rearguard dashed across the road. Volunteer George Fullerton was wounded, but managed to make it across the bullet-swept roadway.

The three remaining men, Commandant Mallin, James O'Shea and Mick Kelly, prepared to make the final run. As they left the gate all hell was unleashed as a barrage of machine-gun and rifle fire was directed at the running figures. Bullets exploded around them as they ran the gauntlet towards the College. They managed to get across the street into York Street, where the crowd of onlookers tried to rush at Mallin with the intention of tearing at him. With his bayonet fixed, O'Shea lunged at the women but Mallin knocked the weapon upwards. They hammered on the side entrance of the College, and Sergeant Robbins opened the door and admitted the men. Commandant Mallin immediately inspected the defences and ordered a section of men onto the roof to reinforce those who were engaging the British posts.

Commandant Mallin had a bullet hole drilled through his hat. His cap badge, the Red Hand badge of the union, had made a tempting target for one of the British marksmen. He took the badge off his hat and presented it to Madeleine Ffrench-Mullen as a macabre souvenir.

The men were exhausted, and many of them collapsed onto floor of the College. Mallin's unit had suffered just four men killed, one seriously wounded and a number with superficial wounds. A makeshift infirmary was set up, and the Cumann na mBan personnel immediately began patching up the wounded and administering general first aid to those who had been hit in the crossing. Many of the Volunteers replenished their ammunition bandoliers before they were assigned posts within the building.

The prisoners that had been taken in the Green had been left in the park – all except Laurence Kettle, who had been brought into the College. Commandant Mallin ordered the prisoner to be kept under guard, as he believed that Kettle still might come in useful at a later date. Sergeant Robbins put Kettle to work reinforcing the window barricades of the College. Regardless of their individual experience, the Irish Citizen Army garrison were all shattered by the horror of the day, emotionally dazed and physically exhausted, and were now trying to make some sense of what had just happened:

> I fell fast asleep, lying face down with my rifle pointing to
> the Shelbourne Hotel. I had only two hours' sleep out of

a period of sixty hours' duty, and that was on the roof of the College of Surgeons on Monday night.[25]

Outside, the gun battle grew in intensity as Captain Elliotson directed the machine-gunner in the Shelbourne to open a sustained fire on the College of Surgeons. From their vantage point on the fourth floor they could see chips of masonry flying in all directions as the bullets impacted. Elliotson moved from room to room checking on the progress of his men. The haze of battle and the stinging, pungent fumes of gun smoke clung in the air as each soldier fired round after round. The early morning assault had released the pressure the men had felt, and they were glad to be finally in action. His unit had sustained some casualties, but the majority were fine and in good spirits. The staff and guests within the hotel administered basic first aid to those who had been hit. The injured were made as comfortable as possible in rooms to the rear of the building.

On the roof of the College of Surgeons, a makeshift firing step had been constructed that enabled the Volunteers to lie flat and take up a more comfortable firing position. Weapons were brought to bear on the British positions. Margaret Skinnider took up position on the roof:

… I climbed up astride the rafters, and was assigned a loophole through which to shoot. It was dark there, full of smoke and the din of firing, but it was good to be in action. I could look across the tops of the trees and see the British soldiers on the roof of the Shelbourne. I could also hear the shot railing against the roof and wall of our fortress, for in truth this building was just that. More than once I saw the man I aimed at fall.[26]

Nearby, incoming rounds disintegrated the window frames of the United Services Club as bullets splintered the wooden surrounds of the sash windows. The window-panes shattered, showering the small garrison with shards of glass. The Lewis machine-gunner balanced the weapon on the sill and engaged the Volunteers on the roof of the College. Spent cartridge cases littered the floor as bullets were ejected from the machine-gun and rifles, which were keeping up a terrific rate of fire against the insurgents in the College. Their mouths were parched, and they were running low on water, having emptied their water bottles during the fight. One soldier gathered the bottles and rushed downstairs to refill them from a tap in the basement kitchen. On his return the soldiers drank greedily from the bottles, as many had nothing to drink since the gun battle began and theirs mouths were parched. The battle continued unabated. The insurgents were cornered, but not about to surrender.

Chapter 9

Tuesday 25 April, 1916: The Best Laid Plans

Having consolidated his position, Commandant Mallin established a Command Post within the College and planned a counter-attack that would infiltrate the British perimeter on the north side of the park.

He detailed a section to carry out an attack and ordered them to prepare to move out. The plan was to occupy Sibley's bookshop on the corner of the Green and Grafton Street, and set fire to the adjacent buildings. Under the cover of the inferno, they were to rush the United Services Club and eliminate its defenders. In order to get to the bookshop, the Volunteers would have to run the gauntlet of machine-gun fire from the College to the top of Grafton Street. Mallin realised that this desperate action would have to take place under the machine-guns of the

British posts and that he would sustain casualties in getting his men into position. The plan had to be abandoned at the last minute as communications between those taking part in the sortie and those providing covering fire broke down. The unit that was to provide covering fire had opened fire before the assault group was in position, thus alerting the British that an attack was imminent.

Margaret Skinnider suggested an attack on the Shelbourne Hotel. This assault would involve cycling past the British positions and lobbing hand-grenades through the windows. Mallin rejected the idea, as the road was a killing zone.

Throughout the College, men and women lay on the floor exhausted, trying to catch some rest. Many of them had not slept for twenty-four hours and had no opportunity for a meal or hot drink. Much of the food and medical supplies had been left behind in the park, and what provisions remained were rationed out. Despite these setbacks, morale was high:

> To those who have been following the Great War, reading of thousands and hundreds of thousands attacking one another in open battle or in mile long trench warfare, this exchange of shots between two buildings across a Dublin green may seem petty. But to us there could be nothing greater. Every shot we fired was a declaration to the world that Ireland, a small country but large in our hearts, was demanding independence. We knew that all over Dublin, perhaps by this time all over Ireland, other groups like ours were filled with the same intensity, the same determination, to make the Irish Republic, no matter how short lived, a reality of which history would have to take account.

Besides, the longer we could keep the tricolour flying over the College of Surgeons, the greater the chance that Irish courage would respond and we should gain recruits.[27]

Within the College, the Volunteers began to settle in to their position. An accidental discharge of a weapon resulted in the wounding of Volunteer Daniel Murray. James O'Shea wrote:

There were a few more casualties. One happened while I was resting; a Howth gun went off and the bullet hit the floor and caught one of the men in the eye. I think he was removed to hospital where he died.[28]

Murray was removed to St Vincent's Hospital, where he died two weeks after the Rising. He was thirty-two years old and came from Rathmines.

In order to attack the British posts, Mallin knew he had to move his men nearer to the British positions without exposing them to the heavy fire from the buildings on the north of the Green. In order to achieve this it was decided to mouse-hole (tunnelling from one house to another without exposing one's troops to enemy fire in order to keep casualties to a minimum) through the buildings adjacent to the College. A section was assembled and equipped with extra ammunition, breaching tools and grenades. With Vice Commandant Markievicz as a guide, the breaching party made their way onto the roof of the College. In order to get from the roof of the College to the roof of the adjacent building, a wooden plank was stretched across a thirty feet drop linking the College roof to that of the Turkish Baths alongside. Many crawled over on their hands and knees trying not to look down at the street below. Balancing a rifle, sledgehammer and a number of grenades, O'Shea ran across the narrow plank. The squad began to breach the walls, tunnelling from one building to another. Another unit under the command of Captain Richard McCormack was detailed to move out from the rear of the College and make their way to the buildings on South King Street and work their way back towards the group that was tunnelling from the baths. Captain McCormack assembled his men and moved out through the rear of the College. A scout moved ahead, cautious that the British could have already occupied the area towards which they were moving. It was important to reach their objective and secure it before Crown forces had the same idea. This plan would enable the task of securing the whole perimeter to be carried out in a shorter time span.

> The reason for this operation was twofold. The first was that we should occupy these new positions and thus forestall a similar move by the British forces. The second was that we planned to operate from the top of Grafton Street and the north-side house of Stephen's Green with the aim of checking the activities of the British forces in the area.[29]

On arriving at the houses on King Street South, doors were kicked open and the Volunteers poured inside their first building. They immediately began barricading the doors and windows with sideboards, chairs, wardrobes and bedsteads. Volunteers took up firing position on the upper floors while others searched for provisions. Presses were raided, and any food that was discovered was distributed amongst the men. Bottles of liquor were sent back to the College for use in the medical bay. The Volunteers then began mouse-holing from building to building.

On breaching an entry into one house, the Volunteers found themselves in the Alexandra Ladies' College. The terrified staff thought the armed force was invading Germans. Noticing a set of Rosary beads wrapped around the wrist of a Volunteer, a young servant girl exclaimed with jubilation, 'They're Catholics!' They managed to acquire a ham from the Ladies College, which was distributed amongst the garrison.

Commandant Mallin took up position beside a shattered window and drew his Mauser automatic pistol. This weapon was fitted with a 'stock' that converted the weapon into a carbine. He fired at an unseen enemy, and his shot was immediately answered, the bullet whisking by his head. He took aim again and fired, exclaiming 'Got him!' A British sniper had come across the Green and had taken up position at the railings opposite the College.[30]

Though his garrison was spread thinly between the College and the houses adjacent to his Command Post, Mallin had managed to secure his perimeter. The rear of his position was still protected by the Irish Volunteers in Jacob's Biscuit Factory. Lieutenant Jackson with a company of men relieved Sergeant Robbins and Captain McCormack and his unit at the South King Street end of St Stephen's Green. Many of the exhausted Volunteers were hungry, having had little or no food since Monday. Nellie Gifford, a trained cook, established a cookhouse within the College of Surgeons and distributed bowls of porridge, which were devoured ravenously.

The British machine-guns had stopped firing, but sporadic sniper fire erupted throughout the night. The soldiers within the hotel rested and ate their rations, which were supplemented by some foods from the hotel's pantry. Captain Elliotson rested some of his platoon while others took watch. A stock of the ammunition was taken and the machine-gun was cleaned and oiled, ready for the morning hate. The soldiers from the 10th Royal Dublin Fusiliers, who had been in the hotel since early on Monday, were sent back to the Castle. Lieutenant Grant returned with the men and submitted a 'sit rep' to Major Price.

The garrison within the United Services Club was nearer to the Irish position and was subjected to intermittent sniper fire from the roof of the College. The men clung on to their position, returning shot for shot against the Irish Volunteers. The Lewis machine-gunner had ceased firing in order to clean and service the gun. Guards were posted in case of an attack as others sat on the floor eating their rations of Bully beef and hard biscuits, discussing the events of the previous day. Tired and weary from being in combat, many of them settled down for the night to grab whatever sleep they could. The soldiers could hear in the distance the fire fights that were raging throughout the city as British forces engaged the numerous posts of the Irish Volunteers. The struggle would continue tomorrow.

Chapter 10

Wednesday 26 April, 1916: Holding Out

At 03.45 hours, British troops opened fire. Machine-gun and rifle fire was directed at the College of Surgeons and at the block of houses that the Volunteers had occupied to the west of the Green. The morning 'hate' as it was called was the practice of firing at the enemy just before dawn, and was standard military practice ever since the cannon had been invented. It's good for morale, and puts the attacking troops on a higher footing and keeps the enemy on edge. The onslaught lasted fifteen minutes before a cease-fire was ordered.

Commandant Mallin's garrison was awoken by a hail of gunfire as machine-gun and sniper fire sent bullets smacking violently into the walls of the College and the buildings on their perimeter. As the shooting died down there was a knock on the side door of the College. Elizabeth O'Farrell and Julia Grenana arrived from the General Post Office with despatches sent by James Connolly. They also brought sacks of bread. The women had a difficult time crossing the city, avoiding British patrols and the hostile crowds of separation women. With the sacks over their shoulders, many people had thought that they were looters and left them alone. This cover provided them safe passage for some of the way. They met Francis Sheehy-Skeffington who recognised them and offered them assistance. Two young boys were given a half a crown each and to carry the loads to the College. They reported on the situation within the city, passing on that morale among the headquarters garrison was high. Commandant Mallin wrote a number of despatches and sent them back with the women.

Within the upper levels of the College of Surgeons, the walls were adorned with paintings of former presidents of the College. Among these portraits hung a painting of Queen Victoria. A young member of the Irish Citizen Army stepped forward, drew a small knife and ripped the canvas from its frame exclaiming 'This'll do for leggings.' On discovering the vandalised painting, Commandant Mallin shouted, 'If we find the man who did that I'll shoot him!' The young boy stepped forward and apologised, only to receive a clip around the ear from the officer.

The houses occupied by the Volunteers on the corner of South King Street and St Stephen's Green West were subjected to sniper fire as British snipers zeroed in on the buildings.

The Volunteers holed up in these posts realised that this threat had to be eliminated.

Mick Donnelly and Mick Kelly, who were with me in the front room, decided that the firing was not coming from an angle but straight from the front. Kelly started to watch for any flash of light in front. There was a slight lull, and away in the distance, three or four houses to the left of Iveagh House, a match flashed as someone lit a cigarette. Donnelly and Kelly fired, and after that we had some peace except for machine-gun bursts every now and again.[31]

Within the Shelbourne Hotel, Captain Elliotson toured his position, checking defences and encouraging his men. Intelligence reports enabled him to organise his defensive strategy:

A good deal of useful information reached us by phone and letter from sympathetic loyalists, and most of it was confirmed by bullets coming into the hotel windows from the direction indicated every day.[32]

The action had been reduced to fighting a careful defensive machine-gun and sniper battle against the Volunteers. The Volunteer posts at the top of Grafton Street were subjected to continuous sniper fire from British positions. It was imperative that they were found and neutralised.

For an hour we could not locate the firer, but with the aid of glasses, Kelly discovered the sniper at the shop next to Sibley's. There were two women at the window at times, but when it was vacant, we got hell. When the ladies appeared again, all was quiet. This had been going on all morning and it was only by chance that Mick Kelly kept his glasses trained on the window. At last he discovered that one of the 'ladies' was a gentleman wearing a blouse. He discovered it as the 'lady' was going back from the window for sniping. The next time the window opened there was only one 'lady'. I watched as Mick fired and shot him. The window came down with a smack and there was no more trouble from that quarter.[33]

A warning was given that a platoon of British soldiers was attempting to work their way up South King Street. A brief gun battle erupted and forced the soldiers to retreat, taking their dead and wounded with them. Within the Ladies' College a telephone rang, and as a Volunteer went to pick up the receiver Captain McCormack wrestled it from him and both men dived for cover as a burst of machine-gun fire smashed the windows and walls of the room. The squad lay on the floor of the room for almost an hour until the firing stopped.

One of the most bizarre incidents of that week was the twice-daily truce that was observed by both sides as Mr James Kearney, the park keeper, entered the Green to feed the ducks.

Late on Wednesday night, Captain Elliotson received information that the Irish Volunteers were intending to reoccupy the Green and launch an all-out attack against his position.

We brought the gun down to the Mezzanine floor commanding the door, and the whole detachment got no sleep that night. They were all on duty, but beyond the fact that a party of cyclists came down the road and disappeared when fired on, nothing happened.[34]

Soldiers from both sides suffered fatigue, their nerves fraught from lack of sleep and the continuous gun battles that had engaged them since Monday. The men settled down for the night, cradling their weapons and trying to get some sleep. However, the latter seems to have eluded many as the odd crack of rifle fire or the burst of machine-gun fire in the distance kept them alert throughout the night.

Chapter 11

Thursday 27 April, 1916: Desperate Measures

At dusk, a Company of British soldiers of the Royal Irish Regiment from Portobello Barracks moved rapidly into position on St Stephen's Green South. Soldiers climbed onto the roof of the University Church and set up a Lewis Machine-gun post. Snipers took up firing positions in the adjacent buildings.

At dawn, rifle and machine-gun fire opened up on the Volunteers' positions and continued throughout the day. In order to neutralise these new British posts, Commandant Mallin decided to send a sortie out that evening in order to remove the threat from this direction.

Margaret Skinnider and William Partridge were detailed to lead a section towards the Russell Hotel on the corner of the Green and Harcourt Street. Here they were ordered to gain entry, work their way down the row of buildings and set fire to the British posts. This would remove the snipers, force the withdrawal of the military and deny this position to the enemy.

At the York Street entrance to the College the section locked and loaded their weapons. Exiting from the side door, they ran in small rushes, keeping tight to the buildings towards the bottom of Harcourt Street.

A shop adjacent to the hotel would enable them to gain access to the roof, and from here they could launch their assault against the British position.

Leaving the cover of the buildings, they careered across the road towards the shop. In order to gain entry, Partridge smashed the glass front of the premises with the butt of his weapon. As the sound of breaking glass echoed throughout the street, a volley of rifle fire erupted from a nearby building. Margaret Skinnider turned to speak to Fred Ryan when he caught the full blast of the first volley of fire, killing him outright. Fred Ryan resided on High Street and was seventeen years old. His death left a mother, an invalid brother and a seven-year-old nephew.

Another volley hit Skinnider, and she collapsed on the roadway. The others threw themselves onto the ground or took cover in the shop doorway. Skinnider's body was dragged into cover as the section laid down a covering fire. She was still breathing, but seriously wounded.

Realising that his position was exposed and the mission had been compromised, Partridge decided to extricate the patrol and fall back to the College of Surgeons. Carrying the body of their wounded comrade, the section fell back towards the College. They could hear the whine of ricochets in the air as they ran. Within minutes they piled in through the door of the College. The sortie had been costly with one killed, Ryan, and one seriously wounded. The Volunteers were ordered to place the wounded Skinnider on a bed in the makeshift hospital where her bloody tunic was removed. Realising that she was badly wounded, and that he did not have qualified medics, Mallin ordered that she was to be taken to the nearest hospital. However, a semi-conscious Skinnider refused to be evacuated and insisted she wanted to remain with the garrison. Margaret Ffrench-Mullen tried her best to stem the flow of blood, applying field dressings to her wounds.

Later that evening, another search of the College resulted in the discovery of the Officer Training Corps arsenal hidden in one of the many rooms that made up the internal labyrinth of the building. Sixty-four rifles with bayonets and a large quantity of ammunition were distributed amongst the garrison.

Food was still scarce, and continued to be rationed. Many of the Volunteers collapsed at their posts from lack of sustenance and had to be removed to the sick bay. Commandant Mallin detailed a unit to go through all the buildings in his perimeter and search for supplies. This resulted in some finds, but the lack of food was to remain a problem in the coming days.

Captain Elliotson ordered a number of men to prepare for a sortie into St Stephen's Green. Weapons were checked and loaded as his men made ready. The soldiers rushed out the side door of the hotel and across the road to the park railings. They scaled the perimeter fence and waited for a moment to see if their presence in the park would draw fire from the College. All was silent as the men moved further into the Green. They picked up an assortment of weapons and ammunition, foodstuffs and medical supplies. They released a number of prisoners who had been held under lock and key in one of the greenhouses. Having carried out a thorough reconnaissance of the park, they retraced their steps and returned to the hotel.

Captain Elliotson questioned the detainees in relation to the strength of Mallin's command and how they were armed. Having been incarcerated for a number of days without food or water, the hotel staff provided a meal for the released internees.

By 12.00 hours on Thursday, Brigadier General W.H.M. Lowe had almost 16,000 troops in position to retake the city. By means of fighting patrols, General Lowe had identified all the Volunteer posts within the city. His plan consisted of raising a cordon around the city and isolating the Volunteer Headquarters at the General Post Office. By concentrating his forces there, he could destroy the control point of the Rising. Other Volunteer outposts could be bypassed and taken later. With the use of artillery, he planned to bombard Volunteer positions into submission. He immediately ordered his men to begin operations and close down the city.

Commandant Mallin asked Christine Caffrey to try and get through to the GPO with a despatch. She left the College and made her way through various side streets towards Dame Street. She had not noticed that she had been followed by a group of unfriendly locals who, on coming upon a British patrol, denounced Caffrey as a spy. She was taken to Trinity College under guard, where she saved herself by swallowing the despatch. One of the officers noticed that she was chewing something, and wanted to know what she was eating. She at once produced a bag of sweets and offered him one. The officer refused her offer very abruptly and informed her that she was going to be searched. She protested, and was subjected to a thorough search by the male officers. When they failed to find any incriminating evidence she was released. She made her way back to the College, where upon entering she fainted. On recovering consciousness she reported her failure to break through British lines. She explained what had happened to Mallin, who replied 'You have done very well.'

The College of Surgeons was now completely cut off.

Since early morning, the inhabitants of Dublin city could hear the unmistakable sound of artillery fire intermingled with the rattle of machine-gun fire. As the day progressed the bombardment grew in intensity. The thud of shells could clearly be heard around the quays and in the vicinity of Sackville Street. A battery of four Royal Field Artillery eighteen-pounders, from the Reserve Artillery Brigade, had been entrained from Athlone. Having cleared small pockets of resistance on the outskirts of the city they were now concentrating on Volunteer headquarters, the General Post Office on Sackville Street. Plumes of black smoke rose into the air and blotted out the horizon. In the ensuing destruction, buildings caught fire and the smell of burning wood, metal and flesh polluted the air.

That night, from their vantage point on the roof of the College of Surgeons, the Volunteers watched the Dantean scenes of mayhem and destruction as the second city of the empire burned.

Chapter 12

From Final Days to the Final Hours

Friday passed with the usual duals between machine-gunners and snipers.

> The British fire would reach a climax, ease up for a short while and then resume again. Sometimes the machine-gun fire would be extremely heavy, and it was our surmise that our snipers had registered hits on such occasions and this was by way of enemy retaliation.[35]

From their positions around the Green, both British and Republican forces could hear a considerable amount of fighting coming from Sackville Street and its environs. By evening, clouds of black smoke rose from the burning embers of Dublin, a heavy black veil that concealed a dead city.

Captain Elliotson and his command were exhausted after a weeklong gun battle against the Irish Citizen Army. The officer had received the comforting information that a secure line had been established from Dublin Castle to Trinity College. The British Army was using the central location of the College for their assault on the General Post Office, and the grounds were filled with hundreds of soldiers waiting to launch an attack against the Volunteer positions. Ammunition had been re-supplied to the hotel garrison from Trinity College via Kildare Street.

Sporadic rifle fire emitted from the shattered windows of the United Services Club. Many of the soldiers lay on the floor, exhausted and hungry. Incoming rounds forced the small garrison to be wary of exposing themselves for too long at the windows. The threat of an all-out assault on their position still remained, and while some soldiers managed to grab some sleep, others watched the approach to the building, hoping that an attack would not materialise.

Within the College of Surgeons, Commandant Mallin walked from post to post, examining the defences and talking to his men. Food was still in short supply, and exhaustion had overcome many as Mallin and his officers tried to rotate sentry duties. Bursts of machine-gun fire forced his men to lie on the floor as plaster dust and glass fragments imploded throughout the many rooms his men occupied.

It was difficult to judge how long the Irish Citizen Army could hold their position. The option of a breakout still remained, but no orders had been received from Command Headquarters, so all he could do for now was hold on and await further instructions. Whatever the case, he would be ready.

Tunnelling continued in the hope of discovering a food supply. A pastry shop was located between the College of Surgeons and the Turkish Baths. On breaching an entry, supplies were sent back to the College. News also reached the garrison that supplies had been sent from Jacob's Biscuit Factory, so the tension caused by the food shortage eased and morale improved considerably.

At 15.45 hours on Saturday 29 April 1916, Headquarters Command of the Irish Volunteers and the Irish Citizen Army had withdrawn from the GPO having endured hours of artillery bombardment. Surrounded by Crown forces, they had managed to relocate their command post to a block of houses on Moore Street. Outnumbered and outgunned, Patrick Pearse decided to surrender his force. James Connolly reluctantly accepted Patrick Pearse's surrender order and amended the instruction for his own force.

At 11.00 hours on Sunday morning, Nurse Elizabeth O'Farrell, a member of the Republican Headquarters garrison, was seen approaching the College of Surgeons under a white flag. Soldiers from both sides watched as the solitary figure walked towards the building, each spectator apprehensive that a single shot might ring out, killing the messenger. She gained entry to the College via the side door on York Street. She asked to see Commandant Mallin, but was informed by Vice Commandant Markievicz that he was asleep. Nurse O'Farrell handed over a typed message indicating that Headquarters Command of the Republican forces had surrendered and that they were to do the same. Mallin was roused from his slumber and read the message in silence. No formal reply was given, and O'Farrell returned to her British military escort.

The Commandant discussed the situation with his officers, and while many were in favour of a breakout, they came to the unhappy conclusion that they must obey orders and surrender as a disciplined force.

Word was sent to each post on the Volunteers' perimeter that a meeting was to be held in the hall of the College. The men and women assembled in the lecture hall, and Commandant Mallin stepped forward and addressed the garrison. He stated that General Headquarters had surrendered and that all Irish Volunteer and Citizen Army posts were to do the same. The garrison objected strongly. Mallin silenced them, saying that 'As soldiers we came into this fight obeying orders. We will now obey this order by James Connolly to surrender.' Permission to do so was granted to those who wanted to escape, and a number of men and women discarded their uniforms and managed to slip away dressed in civilian clothing. The tricolour was hauled down and a white flag was run up the flagpole. Major de Courcy Wheeler, who was staff Captain to Brigadier General Lowe, was assigned to accept the surrender of the Garrison at the College of Surgeons.

… I went to the Castle and obtained information from the Garrison Adjutant that a telephone message had been received from the O.C. Troops, Shelbourne Hotel, stating that the Republican flag over the College of Surgeons had been hauled down and that troops were required to take over the College and the surrender of the Garrison.

I motored back at once to Trinity College and ordered the officer in charge of the military escort, which was in waiting, to proceed up Grafton Street as far as possible and to keep his men out of view of Stephen's Green as there was still sniping from various points.

From there I motored to the Kildare Street entrance to the Shelbourne Hotel and interviewed the O.C. Troops, who pointed out the position from the top of the window where he had his Maxim gun placed.

Having ordered him, and telephoned the O.C. Troops in the United Services Club, not to open fire under any circumstances as I was about to receive the surrender of the garrison, I returned to Grafton Street, picked up the Sergeant Major and drove to the front door of the College of Surgeons.

I ordered the Sergeant Major to bang on the door, and after I waited for a reasonable time without getting any response, a civilian signalled that there was something going on down in York Street. I went there and saw a white flag hanging out the side door of the College. Two of the officers came out, advanced and saluted.

The Commandant stated that he was Michael Mallin and that his companion was Countess Markievicz and that he and his followers wished to surrender … Commander Mallin was not armed but carried a walking stick, which he gave me as a personal memento.[36]

O'Shea recalls the moment Major Wheeler entered the College:

Major Wheeler came in accompanied by another officer. We were standing at ease. Commandant Mallin called us smartly to attention, gave us 'arms down, three paces backward, march', turned about, drew his sword and presented it, haft first, to Major Wheeler.

Major Wheeler asked Mallin were all his men here? When Mallin replied that they were all here, Major Wheeler was surprised as he thought there would be about two hundred. He then told us to get blankets, as we might need them. We were then formed in twos and marched out of the College.[37]

According to British military records, Mallin's Garrison numbered one hundred and nine men and ten women. Although a number of posts throughout the city continued to hold out for another few hours, the fall of the General Post Office marked the end of all organised resistance. The Rising had ended.

Flanked by guards, the small column of prisoners marched towards Dublin Castle.

At the head of the column were Commandant Michael Mallin and Madame Markievicz, who looked very picturesque in that strange and rare scene by the fact of her attire. She was dressed in an Irish Citizen Army tunic, a pair of riding breeches and puttees and a lady's hat with an ostrich feather around the band, part of which showed slightly over the top. Hundreds of people from around the vicinity were standing about; some out of curiosity, a small number sympathetic towards us, but the vast majority openly hostile.[38]

Smoking and talking were forbidden, and these rules were enforced at the point of a bayonet. The anxiety over what would happen next was overshadowed by the sense of extreme disappointment. They had all embarked on this operation with such exceptional morale that it was now extremely hard to accept that not only had the Rising failed, but that they were all prisoners and held at gunpoint.

On reaching Dame Street, the column was cursed and jeered by soldiers of the Royal Dublin Fusiliers. Within the Castle grounds the prisoners were searched and questioned and then transferred to Richmond Barracks, where Commandant Mallin and Vice Commandant Markievicz were separated from the main body of prisoners. While the instigators of the Rising were held separately, the authorities processed groups of Volunteers and Irish Citizen Army.

Johnny Barton and a number of detectives were keeping themselves busy, particularly Barton. He did more than his duty when the official military inspection was finished. Even though he was present at the inspection, he came around to the room after it, and stood in front of each one in order to identify those who he considered were officers or people of note … As Johnny Barton stopped in front of Joseph Connolly he opened his conversation by saying, 'What is your name?', though he knew perfectly well beforehand that he was a brother of Séan Connolly's. The next observation was: Séan is dead.' Joe replied, 'He died for his country,' to which Johnny retorted, 'He was a disgrace to his country.' For resenting this insult, Joe was separated from us.[39]

Over a number of days the prisoners were processed and were marched to the docks under guard.

The British officer in charge, riding on horseback, came down the ranks impressing upon the soldiers to carry out instructions and not to waste time with any prisoner who stumbled or fell. It took very little reasoning on our part to understand the full meaning of this order ....[40]

On Sunday night April 30, many of the Volunteers found out that they were to be transported under guard to prison camps in England.

There were probably 300 to 400 prisoners all penned in the cargo hold of the ship. One bucket of water had been placed there, but before half of us had reached the cargo hold the supply of water was exhausted ... Seeing my approach, one of the soldiers immediately halted me. I told him I was seeking water as there was none in the hold, and his reply came quick and sharp, leaving no doubt of his intention. 'You dirty Irish pig, get back in the hold or you won't require any water.' This was rather a shock to me because, generally speaking, the ordinary British soldiers had shown a different attitude during the day towards their prisoners. Most of us then endeavoured to settle down with the object of having some rest, but there was very little space for this purpose. We made all kinds of attempts to be as comfortable as possible under the circumstances. A group of us managed in this way; two sat back-to-back, one at each side, and across our legs lay the head or legs of other colleagues. In that position I went to sleep and did not awaken until the ship arrived in Holyhead early next day, when I was stiff, cold and sore. On looking around before we were taken from the hold of the ship, some very revolting scenes met our eyes. During the trip some of the men had got sick, and, having no room, actually vomited on their nearest colleagues or on themselves.[41]

While many of the prisoners were to endure hell on earth while incarcerated in British prisons, the fate of those imprisoned in Ireland was to be very different.

Chapter 13

May, 1916: Death Waits For No Man

On May 5 1916 Field General Court Martial at Richmond Barracks in Inchicore tried Commandant Michael Mallin. The judges presiding were Colonel E.W.S.K. Maconchy (President), Lieutenant Colonel A.M. Bent and Major E.W. Woodward.

Two charges were levelled against the accused stating that he:

'Did an act to wit did take part in an armed rebellion and in the waging of war against His Majesty the King, such act being of such a nature as to be calculated to be prejudicial to the defence to the Realm and being done with the intention and for the purpose of assisting the enemy.'

'Did attempt to cause disaffection among the civilian population of His Majesty.'[42]

Commandant Michael Mallin pleaded not guilty to both charges. In his defence he stated:

> I am a silk weaver by trade and have been employed by the Transport Union as a band instructor. During my instruction of these bands they became part of the Citizen Army and from this I was asked to become a drill instructor. I had no commission whatever in the Citizen Army. I was never taken into the confidence of James Connolly. I was under the impression we were going out for manoeuvres on Sunday but something altered the arrangements and the manoeuvres were postponed till Monday. I had verbal instructions from James Connolly to take thirty-six men to St Stephen's Green and to report to the Volunteer officer there. Shortly after my arrival at St Stephen's Green the firing started and the Countess Markievicz ordered me to take command of the men, as I had been long associated with them. I felt I could not leave them, and from that time I joined the Rebellion. I made it my business to save all officers and civilians who were brought into Stephen's Green. I gave explicit orders to the men to make no offensive movements and I prevented them from attacking the Shelbourne Hotel.[43]

From experience, Commandant Michael Mallin knew how a British Army court martial convened. While on active service in India in 1898, Mallin was called as a witness in relation to the shooting of a British officer by a local native. Out of fourteen witnesses who were called to give evidence, Mallin was the only person to state that the accused was innocent. However, the defendant was found guilty, sentenced to death and executed.

In his own trial, the defence presented by Mallin to the court was an attempt to deny all knowledge of the insurrection and those who took part, as Mallin knew that any recognition of another combatant would undoubtedly incriminate them in the eyes of the court. By stating that he was not in command, even though he surrendered the garrison to Major Wheeler, it is possible that Mallin was attempting to confuse the court and undermine the statements submitted by the witnesses for the prosecution. It is clear from his surrender at the College of Surgeons that Michael Mallin knew his fate, yet he clearly attempted to state that he had behaved properly as an officer and exonerate his men from any wrongdoing.

Mallin's statement is open to many interpretations, yet his actions of Easter week speak for themselves.

Found guilty and sentenced to death, Mallin was incarcerated in Kilmainham Gaol. One of his last letters from the prison was to his parents:

My Dear Mother and Father,

Forgive your poor son who is soon to meet his death. I am to be shot tomorrow at a quarter to four. Forgive him all his shortcomings towards you – this applies especially to the management of my father's business.

Dear father, forgive me all, and you, dear mother, the pain I give you now.

Pray for me, give my love to Tom, May, John, Bart, Katie and Jack Andrews. They must all pray for me.

I tried, with others, to make Ireland a free nation and failed. Others failed before us and paid the price and so must we.

Good-bye until I meet you in heaven.

Good-bye again. A kiss for you, dear mother. God bless you all.

I have now but a few hours left. That I must spend in prayer to God, that good God who died that we might be saved. Give my love to all. Ask Uncle James to forgive me any pain I may have caused him. Ask Tom Price and all in the Trade to forgive me. I forgive all who may have done me harm. God bless them all.

Good-bye again, Mother dear, and Father, God bless you.[44]

Your loving son,

Michael Mallin

On the eve of his execution, Mass was celebrated within the prison. Many women of the Cumann na mBan sat in the chapel gallery during the service.

We were all brought to Mass in the prison church. We were in the gallery from which we had a view of the altar and the front seat. We were able to see Eamon Ceannt, Michael Mallin, Con Colbert and Séan Heuston, who were kneeling in the front seat. They were the only ones to received Holy Communion, which we thought significant. That affected us all and I began to cry. We craned our necks to try and see more but the wardresses pulled us back. When the Volunteer prisoners were leaving the church those four were the last to leave and they looked up at us and we waved down to Con Colbert, who waved his hand in reply shaking his head up and down as if in farewell. They evidently knew what their fate would be.[45]

Commandant Michael Mallin was executed by firing-squad in the stonebreakers yard of Kilmainham Gaol between 03.45 hours and 04.05 hours on Monday 8 May 1916. He was forty-two years old, and his death left an expectant widow and four children.

General Sir John Grenfell Maxwell issued the following statement in relation to Mallin's execution:

> This man was second in command of the Larkinite or Citizen Army, with which organisation he had been connected since its inception. He was in command of the rebels who occupied St Stephen's Green and College of Surgeons. At those places serious encounters took place and there were many casualties both amongst the military and civilians. He surrendered on the 30th April and was accompanied by a body of 109 rebels all of whom were armed.[46]

As a final act of defiance, Mallin signed his last letters with the title of Commandant, Stephen's Green Command.

Chapter 14

Aftermath

On 9 May 1916, James Connolly, Commander-in-Chief of the Irish Citizen Army was tried, found guilty and sentenced to death by a military court martial. Having been severely wounded during the insurrection, Connolly had been held under guard at the Red Cross facility within Dublin Castle. On 12 May, as Connolly was being prepared to be transported to Kilmainham Gaol, the surgeon who attended the wounded officer stated that, 'at the moment of his execution he would pray for him and those about to shoot him'. Connolly did not ask for nor expect any quarter to be given, and replied, 'Yes Sir, I'll pray for all brave men who do their duty according to their lights.' Connolly, due to his wounds, was tied to a chair to face his executioners. As the shots reverberated around the stonebreakers yard, this bloody chapter in Irish history had come to an end, but another chapter was just beginning.

Vice Commandant Markievicz was also tried by court martial, found guilty and sentenced to death. However, her sentence was commuted to life in prison. She was released on July 17 1917.

She continued the struggle for Irish independence, and in May 1918 she, along with Maude Gonne McBride, Kathleen Clarke and Mrs Sheehy-Skeffington, were arrested and imprisoned. Later that year she was elected to the British House of Commons and was the first female Member of Parliament. She refused to take her seat, and when Dáil Eireann was formed in Dublin, she was appointed Minister for Labour. She died in 1927.

Imprisonment in England affected the lives and health of many of those Volunteers who fought for Irish Independence during that Easter week in 1916. By December of that year a pardon had been issued, and the slow process of repatriating over three thousand prisoners began.

William Partridge, having survived Easter week, was sentenced to fifteen years in prison. Released under the general amnesty he became a prominent Dublin City councillor.

Michael Doherty, shot on the roof of the College of Surgeons, survived his injuries but died during the flu epidemic of 1918.

Margaret Skinnider also survived being shot, writing about her experiences in her work *Doing my Bit for Ireland*. She returned to teaching and died peacefully in 1971.

Captain Christopher Poole decided to retire from the ranks of the Citizen Army in 1919, first gaining employment with the Port and Docks authority and then later with Dublin Corporation.

In the aftermath of the Rising, many British regiments were brought up to full strength and re-equipped in preparation for action on the Western Front.

Lieutenant Charles William Grant of the 10th Royal Dublin Fusiliers was posted overseas, and saw action on the Western Front during the latter stages of the Battle of the Somme. Wounded in action, he spent a number of months in hospital suffering from 'septic poisoning and shell shock as a result of injuries received on active service.' He was demobilised in 1918 and began working as a civil servant in the Custom House in Dublin, and witnessed the burning of the building in May 1921. He then resided in Ulster, having received an appointment to the Northern Ireland Government. Charles Grant died peacefully in 1970.

Captain Carl Elliotson of the 6th Reserve Cavalry returned to his unit, and seems to have disappeared into obscurity. Though Elliotson is mentioned in many works on the Rising, searches of army records have so far failed to produce any military record. It is possible that, as a reservist, he saw no action in mainland Europe and left the army when hostilities with Germany ceased in 1918.

Second Lieutenant Guy Vickery Pinfield was the first British officer to be shot during the Rising. He was hastily buried in a temporary grave in gardens of Dublin Castle along with dozens of other casualties of that week. Most of these bodies were exhumed and buried elsewhere after hostilities had ceased. However, the young officer's body was to remain in his temporary grave until 1966, when it was exhumed and interred at Grange Gorman military cemetery. A plaque in his memory was erected in St Patrick's Cathedral in Dublin, which reads:

To the glory of God and in memory of
Guy Vickery Pinfield, 2nd Lieut. 8th Hussars Special res.

Killed in action during the Irish Rebellion 24th April, 1916
This tablet was erected by his brother officers 10th
Reserve Cavalry Regiment

His death, and those of many other British soldiers who were killed during the 1916 Easter Rising, were to be overshadowed by the Somme offensive in July of 1916.

On returning to Ireland from prison in England, many men and women of the Citizen Army continued the struggle for an independent Irish Republic. While many members left and joined the newly established Irish Republican Army, there were those who believed that the Citizen Army should retain its separate identity.

> The question of the relationship to the Irish Volunteers immediately came up for consideration. The general feeling was that the Citizen Army should have an independent existence and retain its own Constitution, especially the Labour clauses. These clauses asserted that its members must be, when possible, members of trade unions and be ready to work in harmony with organised Labour for the unity of Irish nationhood and the recognition of the rights and liberties of the world's democracies.[47]

It was decided that each organisation would retain its own status, and that if either side were to engage in military activities they were to notify the other. In the aftermath of the 1918 Armistice, the Irish Citizen Army found itself on active service when an American transport vessel, the *Defiance*, anchored in Dublin port. This ship was laden with arms and ammunition destined to be returned from the Western Front to the United States. Though heavily guarded by American Marines, an operation was planned to get as many weapons and ammunition off the ship as possible. Groups of men under the guise of dockworkers boarded the ship and began smuggling the arms off the boat. Within a few days, the haul consisted of fifty-six .45 revolvers, two thousand rounds of ammunition, twenty-four automatic pistols, five thousand rounds of Springfield rifle ammunition and assortment of flare pistols. The Springfield rifles had to be left behind as they were too cumbersome to conceal, but the mission was deemed a success. In the years that followed, a close working relationship between the Irish Citizen Army and the Irish Republican Army was to prove a key factor in the many successful operations that were carried out during the Irish War for Independence. The signing of a treaty with Britain in 1921 divided the Irish Republican Army, the Dáil, Sinn Féin and the Labour movement. Within months, civil war erupted in Ireland. The Irish Citizen Army opposed the treaty, and army records show that one hundred and twenty-five men and eighteen women took part in actions during the Civil War. Many others were already in action in the Four Courts, but they were there as individuals and not under the banner of the Plough and the Stars. After almost eighteen months of warfare, many of the rank and file of the Citizen Army found themselves imprisoned by the newly established Irish Free State. On May 24 1923, the Republicans ordered a cease-fire and the Civil War drew to a close.

Many of the women suffered terribly at the hands of the Free State forces, imprisoned and forgotten by the country they loved dearly. Those who survived imprisonment in places like

Kilmainham Gaol and the North Dublin Union left behind their memories in prison diaries, letters and graffiti, some of which still remains today on their cell walls. They earned their title of 'no ordinary women'.

The force of working men and women, who had since 1913 fought not only against industrial oppression but also for the cause for Irish liberty, vanished back into the tenements and side streets of Dublin City, leaving behind them a proud legacy of heroism and self-sacrifice.

Military Success & Military Failure

The 1916 Easter Rising started to go wrong within the first few hours of the beginning of the operation. The lack of weapons and manpower greatly hindered the implementation of the overall plan of the insurrection. Spread over a large area, the operation became disjointed and broken up, and the fighting from 24 to 27 April took place in a number of isolated locations, mainly within Dublin city. Republican officers were quick to adapt to a changing strategy that in most cases enabled them to hold their positions throughout the city. Commandant Michael Mallin was one of those officers.

There can be no doubt that Commandant Mallin's force was seriously under strength due to the countermanding order that was issued on Sunday 23 April 1916. Though the Irish Citizen Army numbered between two hundred to three hundred personnel, the number estimated to hold the green would have been five hundred. The Irish Volunteers were also under strength, and only a few men could be spared from that organisation to bolster the ranks of the Citizen Army, and this problem greatly hampered Mallin's deployment of his forces during that week.

> In a conversation I had with [Michael Mallin] afterwards, he told me his reason and Connolly's for occupying Stephen's Green. This was his plan. It was intended that at least 500 men would take over this area. It would be barricaded at different entrances, such as Merrion Street and the street at the Shelbourne Hotel and all streets leading on to the Green. It was to be a base, as it had all the necessaries for a base ....[48]

Commandant Michael Mallin was ordered to take and hold St Stephen's Green as a depot area for Republican Forces. This area would have served as a transport depot capable of linking Volunteer commands throughout the city. The Green was a wide open expanse, centrally located within the city, and had the capability of housing hundreds of prisoners as it could be easily secured. In an urban combat environment a fresh water supply is a necessity for combatants, and the planners of the Rising, James Connolly and Joseph Plunkett, ensured that a supply was secured for their forces.

On occupying the park, Mallin's force began to 'dig in' and fortify their posts. This basic course of action is a military axiom as entrenched positions provide better cover during an attack. These positions were camouflaged and could not be seen from outside the park due to the vegetation in and around the area. The process of 'digging in' is a type of defensive action that is still in use today in order to secure an open area.

The plan to occupy a number of outer posts was a covering action that enabled Mallin to establish and secure his position. As soon as this had been done, outer posts were withdrawn to the central command area. This delaying action was carried out with great military efficiency.

The History of the Irish Citizen Army by R.M. Fox states that although the occupation of the Shelbourne Hotel was part of the original plan, it had to be abandoned due to the lack of men. George Norgrove had been detailed to occupy the hotel, but was reassigned to the General Post Office and then to City Hall. Though the Shelbourne Hotel was the highest building on the Green, it may be considered to be a vulnerable post. On considering a position, an officer must take into account a number of factors in relation to the occupation, defence and possible extraction of one's forces from that building. If Mallin had occupied the Shelbourne he would have had to deploy over one hundred troops to secure the building as the rear of this post would have come under the threat of attack from Crown forces in Trinity College. The glass frontage of the building would have also placed his men in a building that was difficult to defend. The possibility of extricating his force would have been complicated by the lack of supporting positions within the immediate area.

Therefore, on being attacked in the Green, Mallin decided to employ a strategy of 'Defence in depth.'

This military strategy seeks to delay rather than prevent the advance of an attacker, buying time and causing additional casualties by yielding space. Rather than defeating the attacker with a single, strong defensive line, defence in depth relies on the tendency of an attack to lose momentum over a period of time or as it covers a large area. A defender can thus yield lightly defended territory in an effort to put pressure on an attacker's logistics, or force a deployment of enemy forces over a larger area. This will cause the attack to lose momentum, and the defender can now mount counter-attacks against weak points in the attacker's lines with the objective of creating a war of attrition that will drive the attacker back to its original starting point.[49]

Mallin chose the Royal College of Surgeons as his fall-back position as this building was more robustly constructed than the hotel. It could easily be defended, and the garrison in the nearby Jacob's Biscuit factory covered the rear of this building. From a military standpoint, an officer must examine a property in terms of how they would occupy, defend and extricate themselves from that post. The Shelbourne hotel was a vulnerable building that could expose Mallin's positions to attack.

Mallin's military experience and his time in the Irish Transport and General Workers Union created a leader whose command procedure differed greatly from that of other officers during the Rising. His actions of Easter week showed that he believed that there was no greater responsibility than leading soldiers in battle. He knew that every decision, whether made on the field or after hours of consideration, would directly affect the lives of those under his command.

Regard your soldiers as your children, and they will follow you into the deepest valleys; look upon them as your own beloved sons, and they will stand by you even unto death.[50]

Mallin was not willing to sacrifice his men needlessly against fortified British machine-gun posts that had an arc of fire covering the front of his position. Any sortie against the Shelbourne Hotel or the United Services Club would have resulted in heavy casualties for the attackers. In his withdrawal from the Park, his command suffered four fatalities out of an estimated one hundred and twenty officers and men; a very low casualty rate.

No military planner would send a small attacking force with the orders to occupy and hold a military installation that had the capability of billeting over three hundred troops, proving that there was never any plan to occupy Dublin Castle.[51]

According to the original plan, it was never intended to occupy Dublin Castle. The reasons given by Séan Connolly were that the buildings were too spread out, and also that it contained a British military hospital. Our O/C explained to us that to occupy it would be very simple, but to retain it would be very difficult with the number of men at our disposal, as we would have to hold prisoners and feed them, and also the sick and injured who were already in the hospital. We had of course carried out mimic attacks on Dublin Castle towards the end of 1915.[52]

Even though there was only a small number of British soldiers on duty that Easter Monday, the occupation of such a large complex would have been impractical. The force would not have been able to cover the many entrances into the Castle, and Connolly's force would have been too thinly dispersed within the grounds to have any significant value.

[James] Connolly told me that the question of the occupation of the Castle was very carefully considered and rejected because it was a big, straggling building requiring a large number of men to hold it, and commanded in some places by higher buildings, which overlooked it ... He emphasised it was very easy to take but difficult to hold.[53]

The actual plan, to capture and occupy City Hall and its surrounding posts, enabled the safeguarding of the establishment of other insurgent positions throughout the city, and with this in mind the plan was actually a success. If a stronger force had been available, the Irish Citizen Army could have held out longer and prevented the Castle from being reinforced and used later that week as a staging area.

The failure by Republican forces to capture or destroy the Central Telephone Exchange at Crown Alley was detrimental to the overall plan of the Rising, as it enabled the British military to request reinforcements that were subsequently sent to the Castle. While there was a plan to destroy the communications infrastructure, this operation became disjointed. An armed squad of Volunteers were sent from the GPO on Easter Monday with the orders to destroy the lines, but the operation was abandoned, as a report stated incorrectly that the building was occupied by the military.

Hospital records reveal that there were forty-four admissions in the area of St Stephen's Green. The majority of these were civilians caught in the crossfire. Military casualties are difficult to determine, as the British government did not issue a separate list for each area. Because of the similarity to the Republican tactics, British Army casualties may be gauged as being the same or lower than that of the Volunteers.

During the 1916 Rising, British forces were faced with the task of capturing a large, well-defended, metropolitan area. Brigadier General Lowe devised the plan of cordoning the city and concentrating on the main insurgent positions, which he identified as being at the General Post Office and the Four Courts.

This strategy proved successful, enabling the main body of British forces to be deployed against the main insurgent strongholds while other areas of operations could be contained and dealt with at a later date.

Captain Elliotson's force within the Shelbourne Hotel opted for the strategy of maintaining a 'holding position' as they had the greater force that could rely on re-supply and reinforcements. On their initial attack they resorted to using 'Blind Fire', which proved successful in removing the Citizen Army from the Park. This tactic involves firing from a position where one cannot see the target and is thus shooting 'blindly'. From the fourth floor of the hotel, one could not identify the Irish posts within the park as the trees lining the park perimeter and the overhanging foliage concealed them. It was hoped that by firing 'blindly' the Irish Volunteers would return fire and reveal their positions, enabling the British forces to direct fire onto them. This tactic proved successful, as it forced Mallin to withdraw from his position.

Both sides employed the use of snipers, who proved to be invaluable individuals who managed to rule entire blocks of buildings, freezing the manoeuvre of the opposing side when artfully deployed. They frequently demonstrated that they could hold down large numbers of opposing troops, and hence became a favourite tactic of the defender and attacker alike.

There can be no doubt that if Mallin had of refused to adhere to the surrender order, Lowe would have, in time, shelled the College of Surgeons into submission. The planners of the Rising never envisaged that Dublin City, the second city of the empire, would ever be shelled. James Connolly underestimated Crown forces, in that he believed that no capitalist government would ever shell a city because of the resulting damage to property. It was a mistake on behalf of the planners of the insurrection that this idea became the tenet of their strategy.

One must remember that there are many imponderables in war, and that nothing can be predicted with any certainty. It is a military truism that no plan survives contact with the enemy. War is about dealing with the unexpected, changing plans, coming up with new strategies and using every skill you have in order to succeed, a concept that every officer and soldier from both sides had to utilise during the 1916 Rising.

Epilogue

The benefit of hindsight enables one to examine the events of Easter week from a unique perspective. In doing so, however, one must imagine oneself in the firing line of command. Utilising the same resources that were available in 1916, one must then make the battlefield decisions that faced British and Irish Volunteer commanders.

Fighting takes a physical, mental and emotional toll. Orders must be followed amid chaos. Plans must be carried out and circumstances may change quickly. Leadership is multifaceted in that it takes a path along many dimensions and perspectives. The one certainty on the battlefield is that no one knows how he or she will react under fire.

In 1916, James Connolly wrote:

> The general principle to be deducted from a study of the example we have been dealing with, is that the defence is of almost overwhelming importance in such warfare as a popular force like the Citizen Army might be called upon to participate in. Not a mere passive defence of a position valueless in itself, but the active defence of a position

whose location threatens the supremacy or existence of the enemy. The genius of the commander must find such a position, the skill of his subordinates must prepare and fortify it, the courage of all must defend it. Out of this combination of genius, skill and courage alone can grow the flower of military success.[54]

If the insurgency had been a success, everything that Mallin did would have been admired. Tasked with the most difficult area of operations, the officer and his men fought with great tenacity. The isolation of each Volunteer position by Brigadier General Lowe has devalued Michael Mallin's contribution to the Rising.

On the battlefield, Mallin took responsibility for the welfare of his men. This above all is perhaps the most important trait a commanding officer can possess. In those moments that require action without hesitation, a commander knows that the difference between survival and the destruction of one's command might be measured in split-seconds. In combat, a soldier's fate may be decided by chance. In the turmoil of battle, amid the death and destruction, how does one persevere, and why? Out of fear, anger or for a belief? In battle, an officer's training and discipline confront the human instinct for survival, enabling them to make split-second decisions that impact on the lives of those around them.

Obedience to orders means that when an order is given it is obeyed without question for the sake of the operation, the safety of all those involved and for the sake of maintaining discipline. As we have seen throughout history, while orders are often reviewed and questioned later, leaders are still held accountable.

Endnotes

Foreword

1 Napoleon I, *Les Cases, Mémorial de Ste Hélene,* Dec. 4–5, 1815

2 Robbins, F., *Under The Starry Plough* (The Academy Press, Dublin, 1977)

3 Various, *Fifty Years Of Liberty Hall, 1909–1959* (Three Candles, Dublin, 1959)

Chapter 2

4 Folan, P., Witness Statement 316 (Bureau of Military History, 1913–21, Dublin)

5 Jeffrey, K., *The GPO & The Easter Rising* (Dublin, 2006) 41–42

6 Connolly, M., Witness Statement 1746 (Bureau of Military History, 1913–21, Dublin)

7 Autobiography of Charles W. Grant, http://grantonline.com

Chapter 3

8 Stephens. J., *Insurrection in Dublin* (Colin Smythe, Gerrards Cross, Bucks, 1992), p. 27

9 O'Shea, J., Witness Statement 733 (Bureau of Military History, 1913–21, Dublin)

10 McHugh, R., *Dublin 1916* (Arlington Books, London, 1976)
11 Stephens. J., *Insurrection in Dublin* (Colin Smythe, Gerrards Cross, Bucks, 1992), p. 34
12 PRO WO 35/69
13 Robbins, F., *Under The Starry Plough* (The Academy Press, Dublin, 1977), p. 88
14 Robbins, F., *Under The Starry Plough* (The Academy Press, Dublin, 1977), p. 89
15 Robbins, F., *Under The Starry Plough* (The Academy Press, Dublin, 1977), p. 91

Chapter 4
16 McHugh, R., *Dublin 1916*, (Arlington Books, London, 1976)

Chapter 5
17 Lynn, Dr K., Witness Statement 357 (Bureau of Military History 1913–21, Dublin)
18 Autobiography of Charles W. Grant, http://grantonline.com
19 Scallon, J.J., Witness Statement 318 (Bureau of Military History 1913–21, Dublin)
20 Lynn, Dr K., Witness Statement 357 (Bureau of Military History 1913–21, Dublin)
21 Autobiography of Charles W. Grant, http://grantonline.com

Chapter 6
22 O'Shea, J., Witness Statement 733 (Bureau of Military History 1913–21, Dublin)

Chapter 7
23 Caulfield, M., *The Easter Rebellion* (Gill & MacMillan, Dublin, 1995), p. 128
24 O'Shea, J., Witness Statement 733 (Bureau of Military History 1913–21, Dublin)

Chapter 8
25 Robbins, F., *Under The Starry Plough* (The Academy Press, Dublin, 1977), p. 107
26 Skinnider, M. *Doing My Bit for Ireland* (Century, New York, 1917), pp. 130-33

Chapter 9
27 Skinnider, M., *Doing My Bit for Ireland* (Century, New York, 1917), pp. 135-40
28 O'Shea, J., Witness Statement 733 (Bureau of Military History 1913–21, Dublin)
29 Robbins, F., *Under The Starry Plough* (The Academy Press, Dublin, 1977), p. 110
30 O'Briain, L., *The Capuchin Annual* (Dollard, Dublin, 1966), pp. 219-36.
31 O'Shea, J., Witness Statement 733 (Bureau of Military History 1913–21, Dublin)

Chapter 10
32 *Irish Life*, Record of the Rebellion May 12 1916
33 O'Shea, J., Witness Statement 733 (Bureau of Military History 1913–21, Dublin)

Chapter 12
34 *Irish Life*, Record of the Rebellion May 12 1916
35 Robbins, F., *Under The Starry Plough* (The Academy Press,

Dublin, 1977), p. 114

36 Mac Lochlainn, P.F., *Last Words* (Dúchas, Dublin, 1990), p. 119

37 O'Shea, J., Witness Statement 733 (Bureau of Military History 1913–21, Dublin)

38 O'Shea, J., Witness Statement 733 (Bureau of Military History 1913–21, Dublin)

39 Robbins, F., *Under The Starry Plough* (The Academy Press, Dublin, 1977), pp. 127-30

40 Robbins, F., *Under The Starry Plough* (The Academy Press, Dublin, 1977), pp. 127-30

41 Robbins, F., *Under The Starry Plough* (The Academy Press, Dublin, 1977), pp. 127-30

Chapter 13

42 PRO WO 71/353

43 PRO WO 71/353

44 Mac Lochlainn, P.F., *Last Words* (Dúchas, Dublin, 1990), pp. 123-24

45 O'Brien, A., & Curran, L., Witness Statement 805 (Bureau of Military History 1913–21, Dublin)

46 Maxwell. J.G, Memorandum 11th May 1916 (Bodleian Library, University of Oxford)

Chapter 14

47 Fox, R.M., *The History of the Irish Citizen Army* (Duffy & Co. Dublin, 1944)

Military Success & Military Failure

48 Robbins, F., *Under The Starry Plough* (The Academy Press, Dublin, 1977), pp. 74-76

49 Johnson, R., & Whitby M., *How to Win on the Battlefield*

(Thames & Hudson, London, 2010), p. 158
50 Sun Tzu, *The Art of War,* translated by John Minford
(Penguin, London, 2005), p. 61
51 Fox, R.M., *The History of the Irish Citizen Army* (Duffy & Co.
Dublin, 1944), p. 149
52 Oman, W., Witness Statement 421 (Bureau of Military
History 1913–21, Dublin)
53 O'Brien, W., W/S 1766 (Bureau of Military History 1913–21,
Dublin)

Epilogue
54 Connolly, J., *Revolutionary Warfare* (New Books Publications,
Dublin, 1968), p. 34

Select Bibliography

Caulfied, M., *The Easter Rebellion* (Gill & MacMillan, Dublin, 1995)

Fox, R.M., *The History of the Irish Citizen Army* (Duffy & Co., Dublin, 1944)

McHugh, R., *Dublin 1916* (Arlington Books, London, 1976)

Mac Lochlainn P.F., *Last Words*, (Duchas, Dublin, 1990)

Rees, R. *Ireland 1905–25; Vol 1. Text and Historiography* (Colour Print Books, Newtownards, 1998)

Robbins, F., *Under the Starry Plough* (The Academy Press, Dublin, 1977)

Stephens. J., *Insurrection in Dublin* (Collins Smythe, Gerrards Cross, Bucks, 1992)

Von Clausewitz, Carl, *On War* (ed. & trans. Michael Howard & Peter Paret, Princeton University Press, Princeton, 1832/1976)

Index

**"As near as one can possibly get to the fighting
without actually taking part."**
An Cosantóir

Also available in the 1916 IN FOCUS series:

Crossfire: The Battle of the Four Courts, 1916
Paul O'Brien

On Easter Monday 1916, Commandant Edward Daly, commanding the 1st Battalion of the Irish Volunteers, occupied the Four Courts and the surrounding area.

Ensconced in a labyrinth of streets, alleyways and tenement buildings, Daly and the Volunteers created a killing ground that would witness some of the fiercest fighting of the 1916 Rising.

Surrounded and outgunned, the Volunteers held their positions and were the last Battalion of the Rising to surrender.

Confronted by such a determined foe, British military forces were forced to rethink their strategy in order to regain control of the second city of the empire.

Crossfire is the true story of one of the bloodiest engagements against Crown forces during the 1916 Rising. It examines the battles that were fought in and around the Four Courts area of Dublin city, and the atrocities that were uncovered on North King Street as the Rising came to an end.

Field of Fire: The Battle of Ashbourne, 1916
Paul O'Brien

On Friday 28 April 1916, the 5th (Fingal) Battalion of the Irish Volunteers under Commandant Thomas Ashe and Lieutenant Richard Mulcahy fought a battle against the Royal Irish Constabulary at Ashbourne in County Meath.

Often neglected in the history books, this rural battle erupted amongst the hedgerows and bóthairíns of Ashbourne, where men found themselves in a savage conflict in which only mobility and quick thinking could result in survival and ultimate victory.

In the second instalment of the 1916 IN FOCUS series, Paul O'Brien investigates this significant engagement and explores the myths that have grown up around it. A complex and bloody affair, the Battle of Ashbourne was an integral part of the Rising, and would also serve as a template for the tactics and strategies employed by Republican forces during the Irish War of Independence to follow…